The Quaker Girl

Andrew Nicklin and Philip Beeson

A Samuel French Acting Edition

FOUNDED 1830

SAMUELFRENCH-LONDON.CO.UK
SAMUELFRENCH.COM

Copyright © 1988 by Andrew Nicklin and Philip Beeson
All Rights Reserved

THE QUAKER GIRL is fully protected under the copyright laws of the British Commonwealth, including Canada, the United States of America, and all other countries of the Copyright Union. All rights, including professional and amateur stage productions, recitation, lecturing, public reading, motion picture, radio broadcasting, television and the rights of translation into foreign languages are strictly reserved.

ISBN 978-0-573-08080-7

www.samuelfrench-london.co.uk

www.samuelfrench.com

FOR AMATEUR PRODUCTION ENQUIRIES

UNITED KINGDOM AND WORLD
EXCLUDING NORTH AMERICA
plays@SamuelFrench-London.co.uk
020 7255 4302/01

Each title is subject to availability from Samuel French,
depending upon country of performance.

CAUTION: Professional and amateur producers are hereby warned that THE QUAKER GIRL is subject to a licensing fee. Publication of this play does not imply availability for performance. Both amateurs and professionals considering a production are strongly advised to apply to the appropriate agent before starting rehearsals, advertising, or booking a theatre. A licensing fee must be paid whether the title is presented for charity or gain and whether or not admission is charged.

The professional rights in this play are controlled by Samuel French Ltd, 52 Fitzroy Street, London, W1T 5JR.

No one shall make any changes in this title for the purpose of production. No part of this book may be reproduced, stored in a retrieval system, or transmitted in any form, by any means, now known or yet to be invented, including mechanical, electronic, photocopying, recording, videotaping, or otherwise, without the prior written permission of the publisher. No one shall upload this title, or part of this title, to any social media websites.

The right of Andrew Nicklin and Philip Beeson to be identified as author of this work has been asserted by them in accordance with Section 77 of the Copyright, Designs and Patents Act 1988

THE QUAKER GIRL

The original musical, with book by James T. Tanner, lyrics by Adrian Ross and Percy Greenbank, and music by Lionel Monckton, was first produced at the Adelphi Theatre, London, on 5th November, 1910.

This revised version has been freely adapted by Andrew Nicklin and Philip Beeson from the original musical.

CHARACTERS

Mrs Lukyn, landlady of *The Chequers Inn*
William, waiter at *The Chequers Inn*
Nathaniel Pym, a Quaker
Rachel, his sister
Phoebe, English maid to Princess Mathilde
Princess Mathilde, an exiled French princess
Captain Charteris, a King's Messenger
Mme Blum, proprietress of La Maison Blum
Lieutenant Tony Chute, of the American embassy in Paris
Jeremiah, a Quaker, servant to Nathaniel
Prudence Pym, the Quaker Girl
Toinette, head fitter at La Maison Blum
Monsieur Larose, Parisian Chief of Police
Mme Diane Lefevre, a Parisian actress
Prince Carlo, a French prince
Monsieur Duhamel, Minister of State
Villagers, Quakers, Shop Girls, Newspaper Reporters, Mannequins, Guests, etc.

SYNOPSIS OF SCENES

ACT I

SCENE 1 An English country village. A June morning
SCENE 2 On the way to Paris (frontcloth). Immediately following
SCENE 3 La Maison Blum. A few weeks later

ACT II

SCENE 1 Prince Carlo's private enclosure at Chantilly Racecourse. A few weeks later
SCENE 2 On the way from the races (frontcloth). Immediately following
SCENE 3 The gardens of the *Pré-Catalan Restaurant*. That evening

MUSICAL NUMBERS

ACT I

Overture

No. 1	Dawn Prelude and Opening Chorus	Villagers and Mrs Lukyn
No. 2	Entrance of Quakers and Double Chorus	Quakers and Villagers
No. 3	My Beloved France	Mathilde
No. 4	A Quaker Girl	Prudence
No. 4A	When a Bad, Bad Boy	Tony and Prudence
No. 5	Tiptoe	Chorus and Principals
No. 6	I'm Living with a Split Personality	Jeremiah
No. 7	Finaletto (Act I, Scene 1)	Ensemble
No. 8	A Runaway Match	Mathilde, Phoebe, Prudence, Mme Blum, Tony, Charteris and Jeremiah
No. 9	Shop Ballet	
No. 10	The Name That You'll Remember	Mme Blum and Larose
No. 11	Ah Oui	Phoebe
No. 12	Barbizon	Mathilde, Charteris, Jeremiah, Phoebe and Mme Blum
No. 12A	Act I Finale	

Entr'acte

ACT II

No. 13	Opening Chorus "At Chantilly" and Mannequin Parade	Company
No. 14	Come to the Ball	Prince Carlo and Guests
No. 15	A Dancing Lesson	Tony and Prudence
No. 16	The Season	Jeremiah and Phoebe
No. 17	Finaletto (Act II, Scene 1)	Ensemble
No. 18	There's Plenty of Love in the World	Prudence
No. 19	Dance	
No. 20	Just a Friend	Tony
No. 21	Tony from America	Prudence
No. 22	The First Dance	Tony and Prudence
No. 23	Moonstruck	Larose and Mme Blum
No. 24	Finale	Ensemble

The vocal score and orchestral parts are available separately on hire from Samuel French Ltd

ACT I

Scene 1

An olde English country village. A June morning

The exterior of The Chequers Inn, which has a balcony, is R; L *is an oak tree, with a bench*

Overture

No. 1 Dawn Prelude and Opening Chorus

As the Curtain *rises, during the Dawn Prelude, Mathilde is standing on the balcony of the inn, looking out across the village. She goes back inside*

A Villager appears from behind the oak tree and beckons other Villagers on from off stage

The Villagers enter in groups, gossiping amongst themselves. Eventually, they all arrive and sing

Villagers	Here, we've such a tale to tell,
	Have you heard about it?
	There's a lady, quite a swell,
	Nobody can doubt it!
Village Men	She arrived a week ago,
	Staying at *The Chequers*,
Village Girls	With a dozen trunks or so,
	Regular three deckers!
Villagers	True it is, you may depend,
	Prudence Pym the Quaker—
	She's the foreign lady's friend,
	Never will forsake her—
	Goes to see her every day,
	Nobody can stop her,
	Though the other Quakers say——

Two Quakers cross the stage

(*Whispering*) Though the other Quakers say
           That it isn't proper!

Mrs Lukyn appears at the inn door with William beside her

1st Villager (*singing*)	There's Mrs Lukyn at *The Chequers*' door.
2nd Villager	She is the party who can tell us more
3rd Villager	She's so obliging—she will not refuse.
Villagers	Here, Mrs Lukyn, have you any news? Have you any news?
Mrs Lukyn	I am not the sort to chatter Though I'm fairly young!
Villagers	So thinks each man!
Mrs Lukyn	On a most important matter I can hold my tongue!
Villagers	No doubt you can.
Mrs Lukyn	So, if I should tell you something Heard, I won't say whence——
Villagers	Of course we know!
Mrs Lukyn	You'll be as silent as a dumb thing, It's in confidence!
Villagers	Just so!
Mrs Lukyn	Gossips all are mischief-makers, Slyly whispering——
Villagers	Yes, that's true!
Mrs Lukyn	You must be as mum as Quakers, Don't repeat a thing!
Villagers	That we won't do.
Mrs Lukyn	I have always hated scandal With a scorn intense——
Villagers	Quite right, we know!
Mrs Lukyn	So whatever now I handle Is in confidence!
Villagers	Just so!

Mrs Lukyn (*speaking*) So, what do you want to know?

Villagers (*together*) { Where's she come from?
What's she doing here?
Has she run away?
What's her name? (*Etc.*) }

Mrs Lukyn (*interrupting*) Now it's no use asking me, you know I never talk about my customers. All I know is that the young lady staying at my hotel *is* a lady, for all she's French.

1st Villager Here, Mrs Lukyn, is it true that she's asked Phoebe, the postman's daughter, to be her maid?

Mrs Lukyn Well, Phoebe's a good girl, and when the young lady asked if I knew anyone suitable, well, I thought of her. Now, I can't stand around here all day chattering to you. William, will you see to it that our two best rooms are prepared.

William More arrivals, ma'am?

Mrs Lukyn Friends of the young lady—she told me she was expecting them when she arrived last week. Oh and she's ordered breakfast.

William Breakfast, ma'am?

Mrs Lukyn (*puzzled*) At twelve o'clock she says, "Dejeunay"—that's French for bacon and eggs, I suppose—"Dejeunay, and wine for the gentlemen".
William Oh, I'm sorry, ma'am. I can't be serving no breakfasts at twelve o'clock. Vicar, he's told me to be in church at half-past eleven to ring the tenor bell.
Mrs Lukyn Then I suppose I'll just have to do it myself as usual. (*Starting to go*) Such goings-on. Anyone would think there was a wedding taking place ... (*She realizes*)
William } (*together*) A wedding!
Mrs Lukyn }
Villagers A wedding!
William Why, that's it of course: clear as day, it's an elopement, right here in our village.
Mrs Lukyn Oh my goodness me. A wedding at my hotel, and breakfast at twelve. I'd best get the silver polished. Twelve o'clock! And listen here—no gossiping! Mum's the word!
Villager Mum's the word!

Mrs Lukyn exits into the inn

William Talking of Mum—here come them Quakers, agoing to their meeting again, I don't doubt.

The Quakers enter, led by Nathaniel Pym and his sister Rachel

No. 2 Entrance of Quakers and Double Chorus

Quakers (*singing*)	While our worthy village neighbours Gossip or resume their labours, From the busy world retreating, We will hold our Quakers' meeting. With our friends and our relations Sit in silent meditations, Not a single word repeating— So we hold our Quakers' meeting!
Village Girls	Why are you looking so glum and blue, Solomon, Solomon Grundy? We have a budget of news for you, Solomon, Solomon Grundy!
Village Men	There have been such goings-on at the inn, Really we hardly know where to begin. Stay for a chat—for it isn't a sin, Solomon, Solomon Grundy!
Villagers	Ah! Why should you stick in your hall all day, Solomon, Solomon Grundy? Passing the time in a foolish way, Nothing to drink nor a word to say! Solomon, Solomon Grundy!
Village Men	Couldn't you leave it till Sunday?

Villagers	Stay and be wise,
	Open your eyes,
	Solomon, Solomon Grundy!
Quakers	Nay, friends, nay!
	Nay, friends, nay!
	We cannot stay!

Villagers Don't be as mum as any mouse	**Quakers** Tho' your gossip and your chatter
When the cat is at her!	May not be a sinful matter,
Leave your stuffy meeting-house,	
That'll never matter!	
We've a lot of news to tell	Worldly pleasures are but fleeting
That'll take some beating;	
So today you might as well	We prefer a Quakers' meeting!
Drop your Quakers' meeting!	
Have a talk and raise a glass	We wish you all enjoyment,
That'll be enjoyment;	
If you want the time to pass	In your profitless employment,
That's the right employment!	
Stay a bit and you will hear	And withdraw with friendly greeting,
Something worth repeating,	
Then we'll leave you, never fear	
To your Quakers' meeting!	To our quiet Quakers' meeting!
We will leave you, never fear,	Our quiet meeting! Our quiet meeting!
To your meeting!	Our meeting!

Nathaniel (*speaking*) Friends, let not our footsteps falter on the way!
William Oh! Mr Pym, the young foreign lady in *The Chequers* be asking to see your niece Miss Prudence. Seems they've struck up quite a friendship.
Nathaniel Say unto the foreign maid, that our niece is even now at the meeting-house yonder wrestling with the spirit within.
William Why, you haven't been and shut Miss Prudence up on a beautiful June morning like this, have you?
Nathaniel She hath been secluded from contamination, friend. Come, the spirit may move us to further admonish our erring niece.

The Quakers exit

William One of these days, they'll push that Quaker lass too far, and she'll be up and away.

Phoebe enters from the inn

Phoebe Oh, William, have you ordered the dejeunay. Oh I'm forgetting you don't speak French. Dejeunay is French.
William (*tongue in cheek*) Oh really. And what is dejeunay, Phoebe?
Phoebe (*stuck for a moment*) Never you mind! There are some things that no gentleman mentions to a lady.

Act I, Scene 1   5

Villager How do you like your new position, Phoebe?
Phoebe Oh, she's a dear is mamselle, and no mistaking.
William Mamselle? And what might that be French for?
Phoebe (*glibly*) That is French for princess. (*She realizes her indiscretion*)
William ⎱ (*together*) Princess?
Villagers ⎰
Villager Well, I've just remembered something I have to do, I'll see you later.

The Villagers run off

Phoebe Come back here! Wait a minute, I didn't mean it . . .
William (*going into the inn*) Mrs Lukyn, ma'am!

William exits into the inn

Phoebe Oh, now I've done it—now it'll be all over the village.

Mathilde enters

Mathilde Phoebe, is there any sign of my guests yet?
Phoebe Not yet, your Highness . . . oh!
Mathilde Phoebe, you must forget what I told you. In England I am no longer a poor Bonapartist princess in exile, but a simple French girl enjoying an English holiday.
Phoebe Oh I do beg your pardon your Highness—I mean miss—I mean mamselle. You're not going to dismiss me are you?
Mathilde No, I'm not going to dismiss you—and if you wish you may stay with me after I am married.
Phoebe Married! What, here in the village? Today?
Mathilde Today! Phoebe, I am to be married not to the prince they chose for me in France, but to a man I have chosen for myself—Captain Charteris.
Phoebe Do you mean you've run away from a prince to marry a captain, mamselle?
Mathilde Captain Charteris is a King's Messenger, Phoebe, the best, the dearest man in the world.
Phoebe So he ought to be to marry you, mamselle.
Mathilde Oh, Phoebe, do run to the end of the road, and see if you can see him.
Phoebe Yes, mamselle. (*She starts to go*) Oh mamselle, you must be the happiest young lady in the world.

Phoebe exits

Mathilde And yet, I have one regret. How I wish I could have been married in my beloved France. (*She sings*)

No. 3 My Beloved France

Over the English Channel,
Back on the shores of France,

There was I born,
Now am I torn
Far from its gay romance.
Avenues lining Paris,
Framed by the trees above,
There would I be,
Over the sea,
There with the one I love.

> In my beloved France
> There where I found romance
> Though I have fled
> There would I wed
> In my beloved France.

How I should love to wander,
Only the moon above,
Back in my home,
Never alone,
Wandering with my love.
Our wedding day breaks slowly;
Dawn comes then sun will shine.
"Dear," I would say,
"Take me today,
This is your realm and mine".

> In my beloved France
> There where I found romance,
> Though I have fled,
> There would I wed
> In my beloved France.
> In France.

Captain Charteris enters

Charteris Mathilde, my darling—my princess.
Mathilde Your exiled princess.
Charteris Ah, they may exile my princess, but not my wife.
Mathilde And when I am Mrs Charteris, I shall no longer be a princess, and I may return to my beloved France.
Charteris You will always be my princess. But how did you manage to get away from the school? Over the garden wall?
Mathilde No, I said I was going to take a "petite promenade", and I came straight here, just as you told me.
Charteris To marry a poor devil of an Englishman, when you might have been the wife of Prince Carlo—with a title, and money and estates.
Mathilde Ah, but you see, I want this poor Englishman, and I don't want Prince Carlo, or his money. But now tell me, did you manage to see Mme Blum while you were in Paris?
Charteris See Mme Blum? Why I've half lived at Maison Blum just so that I

Act I, Scene 1   7

could talk about you. And you know, these days Maison Blum is just about the most famous fashion house in the whole of France.
Mathilde Dear Blum. I'm so pleased. She's been so good to me, so loyal and now she's the only friend I have in Paris. Oh I do wish she were here now. She would curtsy—so—and then say "Princesse".
Charteris But haven't I told you, my darling? She is here.
Mathilde Here? In England? But where?
Charteris About half a mile down the road. Our automobile overheated, but I couldn't wait, so I came on ahead. Chute's looking after her.
Mathilde Chute? Who is Chute?
Charteris Tony Chute. Lieutenant Tony Chute of the American Embassy in Paris. The best friend a chap could have, and my best man. You'll like him a lot.

A car engine is heard approaching in the near distance

The car arrives upstage, driven by a chauffeur, with Mme Blum and Tony, who is holding her two poodles, in the back. During the following, Phoebe enters and the Chauffeur unloads several hatboxes and cases from the back of the car

Mme Blum and Tony get out of the car and move downstage

Mme Blum Where is she? Ma petite Mathilde—ma princesse!
Mathilde Blum! Dear, darling Blum!
Mme Blum (*curtsying elaborately*) Princesse!
Mathilde Oh no! No longer princesse, but 'Tilde as of old.
Mme Blum Chérie! Ma petite 'Tilde. And to be married—married to a nobody—a mere captain.
Mathilde Blum.
Mme Blum Oh, forgive me, chérie. He loves you—I would never have given my consent otherwise. And he is so much better than the Prince Carlo.
Mathilde And you have come all the way from Paris to see me married? How is La Maison Blum?
Mme Blum La Maison Blum is the rage of Paris. Wherever I go, people, they say to me "Madame Blum, what will be the next mode?" Ah, who knows, I must await the inspiration! But for you, for the marriage of ma petite, I have brought a Blum création par excellence!
Mathilde Oh, but I was going to be married just as I am.
Mme Blum What? Never! A princesse? C'est impossible—inimaginable—inconceivable—out of ze question!
Tony I don't think she likes the idea.
Charteris Oh darling, this is Chute. My great friend Lieutenant Tony Chute.
Tony Princess, I'm honoured. You'll pardon me if I don't shake hands. (*They are full of Mme Blum's poodles*)
Mathilde Captain Charteris has spoken of you, Mr Chute.
Tony I deny every word.
Mathilde It is very kind of you to have come. Phoebe, would you please give Mr Chute some assistance.

Phoebe takes the poodles into the inn

Tony sits on a pile of hatboxes

Mme Blum (*horrified*) Ah, the wedding costume—it will be ruined.

Tony Pardonnez-moi, chérie. Princess, will you accept a little cadeau-de-noce? (*He gives her a brooch. To Mme Blum*) C'est parfait, n'est ce pas?

Mme Blum Ah, c'est le plus beau cadeau que je n'ai jamais vu!

Tony Oh, plume de ma tante, I'm sure!

Mathilde It's beautiful.

Tony Glad you like it.

Charteris Awfully good of you, Chute. I say, it's past eleven.

Tony (*to Mathilde*) He bought a watch in Paris.

Mme Blum Come then, petite. We must prepare ourselves.

Mathilde But I did so want the little Quaker girl to see me married. I'm afraid those horrid relatives of hers have shut her up again.

Mme Blum Quakaire? What is Quakaire?

Mathilde Her name is Prudence. If you see her, dò please ask her to come to the church. You can't mistake her.

Tony I'll have her there with bells on.

Charteris It's—er—it's quarter past eleven.

Tony By the same watch? How time flies!

Mme Blum Come, chérie, and see my finest creation.

Tony hands Mme Blum the hatboxes

Mathilde and Mme Blum exit into the inn

Tony Au revoir, ma belle Pickford. So how much leave do you have for this matrimonial racket?

Charteris Only two days. We'll have to start for Paris. (*He looks at his watch*) Tonight.

Tony You know, I really wish I'd bought one of those now.

Charteris I have to go to the church to see that everything's arranged. Are you coming?

Charteris exits quickly

Tony Hold on—not so fast. We're not all flying on the wings of love!

Tony follows Charteris off. Nathaniel, Rachel and Prudence Pym enter with the other Quakers

Nathaniel Sister, the lost one, our servant Jeremiah, was not at the meeting-house.

Rachel Doubtless he hath been wrestling with the spirit within.

Nathaniel Jeremiah is certainly inclined to things of lightness.

Rachel Indeed, he joineth our niece Prudence in the paths of waywardness.

From the inn there is the clatter of dishes being dropped, followed by a girl's scream

Nathaniel
Rachel } (*together; looking at each other*) Jeremiah!

Act I, Scene 1   9

Jeremiah enters, laughing

Jeremiah I've done it! I've kissed the cook.

The Quakers are horrified

I don't care. I'm only a Quaker on Mother's side, and—well—sometimes Father will out.
Rachel Brother, were it not well that I went to comfort yon handmaiden?
Jeremiah Don't worry. I've seen to that. (*He turns round, and we see that he has floury handprints on his behind*)
Nathaniel Forth from our fold, thou man of wrath!
Jeremiah Man of froth, am I? Here William, bring me a gin and ginger beer. The gin's for Father—the ginger beer for Mother. (*He lights a cigar*) Man of froth am I?
Rachel He smoketh.
Jeremiah I most certainly do-eth. Oh Father's fairly let loose now!
Rachel Brother, come. Let not our eyes witness this spectacle of depravity.
Nathaniel Come, friends, we will turn our backs on the lost sheep.
Jeremiah Bah!

The Quakers exit in procession

Prudence is at the rear and is about to go when Jeremiah stops her

Miss Prudence! They've let you out at last then.
Prudence I have been well content, Jerry.
Jeremiah Content? In the meeting-house?
Prudence Yes, I have found much within this book to beguile the time.
Jeremiah (*taking the book from her*) Reflections.
Prudence It is thus named outside, Jerry, for the sake of convenience.
Jeremiah (*looking inside*) Reflections of a Bright Young Thing.
Prudence Aunt Rachel saw the outside title, and said she hoped I would gain much profit by it. I have.
Jeremiah Listen, Prudence. I've made a momentous decision. I'm going to run away.
Prudence Run away? Where to?
Jeremiah I don't know, but now that Father's out on top, I should like to see a bit of life.
Prudence At times, the spirit moveth me that way too. Oh, Jerry, what shall I do without thee?
Jeremiah What shall I do without *thee*, Miss Prudence?
Prudence Thee'll be so repentant tomorrow. Why thou art quite pale and trembling now.
Jeremiah Am I? That's Mother. She always did object to smoking.
Prudence Jerry, wouldst thou run into the inn and tell the young lady that I am here?
Jeremiah Yes, miss.

William enters with a gin and ginger beer

William Here be the gin you ordered, Jerry.

Jeremiah Oh take it back inside, would you, William. (*To Prudence*) I shall "wrestle with the spirit within".

William and Jeremiah go into the inn

Prudence I wonder if Jerry really will run away. I wish I could go too, to somewhere where there is no-one to say "Thee must not do this—thee must not say that". (*She sings*)

No. 4   A Quaker Girl

> Oh, a quiet Quaker maid
>> From my babyhood I've been,
>
> For I never even played,
>> With the boys upon the green;
>
> But I used to sew and mend,
> Whilst my aunt was sitting near,
> Till a little Quaker friend
>> Came and whispered in my ear:
>> "Thee loves me, and I love thee."
>> Oh, he was a young mischief-maker;
>
> Two little sweethearts we used to be—
>> He was such a dear little Quaker!
>
> Now I'm quite a Quaker Girl,
>> Very modest and sedate;
>
> If my hair begins to curl
>> I am told to brush it straight;
>
> And the days are very sad,
>> And the world is very grey
>
> For there's not a Quaker lad
>> Who will come to me and say:
>> "Thee loves me, and I love thee."
>> None to woo a maiden and take her;
>> Nobody seems to care about me—
>> Life is very dull for a Quaker!
>
> But altho' the Quaker men
>> Do not know the way to woo,
>
> I have fancied now and then
>> There are other men who do!
>
> If I meet with one of these,
>> Then it might be very nice
>
> When we walked beneath the trees
>> If he told me once or twice:
>> "I love thee and thee loves me."
>> Love's the only true marriage-maker,
>> Somebody's wife one day I may be
>> But *not* the little wife of a Quaker!

Tony enters

Act I, Scene 1

Tony Hello—a Quaker Girl—wonder if she is *the* Quaker girl. Good-morning! (*He takes off his hat*) Oh! Quaker custom to keep your hat on? (*He puts it back on. Aside*) Better adapt myself. (*Aloud*) Sister, canst give me tidings of a maiden named Prudence?
Prudence Yes, friend. What seekest thou with her?
Tony I would even commune. I am the bearer of tidings. Perchance, or perhaps peradventure, thy name is Prudence?
Prudence Yes—and thine?
Tony To the elect, I am known as Anthony, but to friends, Tony. Tony Chute.
Prudence Verily, friend, methinks Tony were better than Anthony.
Tony Then you'll call me Tony, will you?
Prudence Friend, thy manners savour of the world without. (*She starts to go*)
Tony I prithee, do not go. Thee is not—married, Prudence?
Prudence My thoughts have not dwelt on the matters of marriage, friend Tony. (*She goes again*)
Tony Nay, tarry—hath none of the—er—brethren talked to thee of—er—love?
Prudence Nay, it were unseemly—as thou, who are apparently of our persuasion must know. And they are too good to think of love. Art *thee* very good?
Tony Well, I . . . er . . . Dost thee like only those who are very good?
Prudence I have seen none other.
Tony (*aside*) I must have got off at the wrong station! (*Aloud*) And if thee met one who was not so very good, wouldst thou like him?
Prudence Perchance! One waxeth weary of the *very* good sometimes.
Tony Then, Prudence, I will tell thee—I am not so *very* good. Not too good to think of love when I see thee.
Prudence Oh! Then thee must see my uncle and my aunt. They delight in reclaiming the straying ones.
Tony Cannot I persuade *thee* to try? I am yours, Prudence, for the reclaiming.
Prudence Then thee must not think of worldly things.
Tony That's easy. I'll think of you—thee—thou!
Prudence Thee must read much in good books.
Tony Then I will devour thine. (*He takes her book*)
Prudence No! no! You mustn't look, please.
Tony *Reflections!*
Prudence Please—please don't open it.
Tony Certainly not—if you don't wish it!
Prudence Friend—thee are no Quaker.
Tony Why?
Prudence One of our persuasion would have opened and read it.
Tony Well, I admit I'm not a Quaker at present, but I'm quite willing to become one, if *you* want me to.
Prudence But it may be that I would not like thee as a Quaker, friend Tony.
Tony Then why not like me as I am, friend Prudence? (*He sings*)

No. 4A When A Bad, Bad Boy

	When a bad, bad boy like me
	Meets a good, good girl like you,
Prudence	Well, the good little maid
	Is a bit afraid
	And wonders what on earth to do.
Tony	If the bad, bad boy should speak
	Will the good, good girl reply?
Prudence	Well, it rather depends
	If the good girl's friends
	Are anywhere at all close by.
Tony	Such a bad, bad boy!
Prudence	Such a good, good girl!
Both	Oh, they do make a curious pair.
Prudence	Though the good girl may
	Turn her head away,
	Still she knows that the bad boy's there.
Tony	If the bad boy walks
	By her side and talks,
	Will she snub him as a maiden should?
Prudence	Well, I think thee's a lad
	Who is not so very bad,
	And I'm not a bit too good!
Tony	If the good, good girl sits down
	What's the bad, bad boy to do?
Prudence	He must sit over there,
	For the good girl's chair
	Was surely never meant for two.
Tony	If the bad, bad boy comes too close,
	Will the good, good girl be vexed?
Prudence	Well, she might run away,
	Or—she might just stay
	And see what's going to happen next.
Tony	What a bad, bad boy!
Prudence	What a good, good girl!
Both	Oh, they do make a curious pair!
Prudence	If the good girl's wise,
	She will shut her eyes
	When the bad boy begins to stare.
Tony	May the bad boy, please,
	Give her hand one squeeze?
	For he'd like to, if he only could.
Prudence	Oh, I fear thee's a lad
	Who is very, very bad—
	Now really thee must be good!

They dance

Oh, I fear thee's a lad
Who is very, very bad—
Now really thee must be good!

Charteris enters. Prudence makes a fairly hasty exit, leaving her book with Tony

Charteris They're ready at the church! Where is she? Where is the princess? Have you got the ring?
Tony Have I got the ring? Have I known her long enough for that?
Charteris What the deuce are you raving about?
Tony The dearest, sweetest thing on earth. The dear little Quaker Girl.
Charteris Now look here, Chute, don't be a fool!
Tony How you could ever have wasted a moment's thought on Diane and the rest in Paris beats me.
Charteris I? You, you mean!
Tony Same thing.

Mme Blum enters, sobbing

Mme Blum It is useless. I cannot give her to you—ma princesse—ma petite exiled one! (*Waving her arms about*) Non, non.
Tony There's a pigeon loose somewhere.
Charteris Isn't she ready?
Mme Blum Ah, yes, she is ready. But ah—to part with her!

Mathilde enters in an extravagant wedding dress

Mathilde I hope I haven't kept you waiting?
Charteris Oh no! No! How beautiful you look.
Mathilde And all thanks to Blum. Dear Blum. (*She hugs her*) Mr Chute, have you seen Prudence?
Tony Have I seen Prudence? Yes, and I need Prudence.
Charteris Oh, he's hopeless—a sudden attack of *l'amour*.
Mme Blum But you promised to look after me.
Tony That was this morning—early.
Mme Blum Ah, chérie, after this marriage, where will you live? Here in England?
Charteris Later on perhaps. But first we must return to Paris.
Mme Blum (*alarmed*) To Paris?
Charteris Well, yes. I'm on duty there in three day's time.
Mme Blum Impossible. Do you not know that the princess is in exile?
Charteris The princess may have been exiled, but in half an hour she'll be Mrs Charteris, my wife.
Mme Blum It matters not. Within a few hours they would turn my princess out of France again, or worse.
Mathilde Oh, Blum, dear Blum, what is to be done? We can't be separated now.
Mme Blum Oh these children, these children! But yes—I have the inspiration—perhaps there is a way—if you are discreet.

Charteris } (*together*) Yes, what is it?
Mathilde

Mme Blum The princess must put on her most simple costume to travel. Then, if there is any question, I will say that you are one of my employees at Maison Blum. Et, voilà! Husband and wife are together, and I shall have ma petite near me in Paris after all.

Charteris } (*together*) { Bravo!
Mathilde   { Good idea!

Prudence enters

Mathilde Oh, I'm so glad you're here. Prudence, this is Captain Charteris. And this is my friend Mme Blum.
Tony (*turning round*) And this is me!
Mme Blum (*inspired*) Ah, voilà! At last. The inspiration. I will make that the new mode in Paris.
Tony What's that? You're going to make me a fashion plate in Paris? What a colossal idea!
Mme Blum No! No! You are not beautiful. I speak of this—the Quakaire costume: the apron—the collaire—magnifique. It will be the rage. You must come to Paris with me.
Prudence To Paris? Oh, I'm afraid it's out of the question.
Tony (*aside*) Paris? Prudence in Paris? Oh no! Wild oats don't mix with Quaker oats!
Charteris Mathilde dearest ... (*He looks at his watch*)
Tony Same old watch!
Mathilde (*to Prudence*) Will you come to church to see me married?
Prudence I don't think I ought. What would the Friends say?
Mathilde Oh please ... I should so like you to.
Prudence Very well then, but we must go quietly.

No. 5   Tip-toe

Mathilde and Charteris	Tip-toe! Tip-toe! Quietly to church we go; Speak low, speak low! Don't let anyone know.

Villagers begin to enter in twos and threes

Mathilde **Charteris**	Tip-toe! Tip-toe! Step as light as falling snow Just so, stealthy and slow, On tip, tip-toe!
Mathilde	We're in breathless expectation, Ready for our celebration, That is now to crown our daring plans!
All Principals	Our daring plans!
Mathilde	But I'm all in trepidation, Lest some prying male relation Should, as you would say, forbid the banns!

Act I, Scene 1   15

Villagers	Tip-toe! Tip-toe!
	Like a noiseless shadow-show,
	Just so, silent and slow,
	On tip, tip-toe!
Prudence	Though they laugh
	Light and merrily,
	I am half
	Frightened verily!
	And in fact
	Faint with alarm.
Tony	Let me offer my arm!
Prudence	Our sedate
	Friends' Society,
	Reprobate
	As impiety
	Such an act—
	So if they see——
Tony	Thee refer them to me.
Villagers	Tip-toe! Tip-toe!
Mathilde	Don't you let anyone know.
Villagers	Tip-toe! Tip-toe!
Mathilde	Don't you let anyone know! ah!
Villagers	Tip-toe! Tip-toe!
Tutti	˙Tip-toe! Tip-toe!
	Quietly to church we go,
	Speak low, speak low
	Don't let anyone know.
	Tip-toe! Tip-toe!
	Tripping two and two in row
	Just so, wary and slow,
	On tip, tip-toe!
	Tip-toe! Tip-toe!
	To church we will go,
	Tip-toe! Tip-toe!
	To church we will go,
Mathilde	To church we'll go!
	To church we'll go!
Mme Blum	Oh please hurry!
Tutti	We will go, tip-toe!

Mrs Lukyn and William watch from the inn as everyone exits, with Tony and Prudence at the rear

Tony (*as they go; speaking to Prudence over the last few bars of music*) How far is this church? I hope it's a long way.

Mrs Lukyn and William come forward

Mrs Lukyn Well, I must say, a sweeter bride I never saw. Reminds me of myself at her age, William.
William Only more so, if I might be so bold, Mrs Lukyn, mum.
Mrs Lukyn Now, William, no compliments, you're old enough to know better.

Phoebe enters

Phoebe The princess says she'd like breakfast "ong plain air", Mrs Lukyn.
Mrs Lukyn Oh dear, now whatever does that mean? Phoebe, you understand French.
Phoebe (*floundering*) It means ...
William Have the breakfast out here, ma'am, foreign fashion, I expect.
Phoebe I was about to say that, William, only I'm not thinking too clearly just now. I've been so busy this morning packing mamselle's truso.
William Truso?
Phoebe *That* is French for trunk. The French lady takes one look at mamselle's box and says "Mong jeur, what a truso!" Now if you'll excuse me, I have to run home and get Mother to pack my tin truso.
Mrs Lukyn William you'd better run along to church if you're to ring the bell.
William Yes, ma'am.

Mrs Lukyn and William exit, Mrs Lukyn into the inn. Jeremiah enters

Jeremiah Phoebe!
Phoebe I'll thank you to be less free with your Phoebes.
Jeremiah But, Phoebe——
Phoebe And what's this I hear about you kissing the cook?
Jeremiah It's only Father's free and easy way. You see I'm always thinking of you ...
Phoebe Well?
Jeremiah And thinking of you makes me feel—well, it wakes up Father—it was him that kissed the cook, Phoebe.
Phoebe Well, in future, you can tell Father to stick to the cook, or the chambermaid, or whoever else he likes—for he shan't kiss me.

Phoebe exits

Jeremiah Aw, Phoebe! Phoebe! That's the sort of trouble I'm always getting into. And it's never my fault! It's Father's, or Mother's, or both! (*He sings*)

No. 6 I'm Living with a Split Personality

Some people see things black and white,
For me it's black and grey.
But sometime's Father's *joie de vie*
Hides Mother's Quaker way.
If only they'd agreed at birth
On what I ought to be,

Then life would be much simpler for
My trouble is you see, that
    I'm living with a split personality,
    Life is very complex you'll agree.
    Sometimes my mother's dominant
    And I behave so well,
    Then Father sees his chance, and
    Good intentions go to . . .
    Somewhere very hot!
    While I'm left standing in the middle,
    Trying neither to offend,
    For I'm living with a split personality
    And no-one knows who'll triumph in the end!
So when it comes to girls and drink
My father says OK.
Then Mother steps right in, convinced
That temperance must pay!
I wish I could be in control
Or very soon I'll crack,
At least I'd know that come what may
My life would all be black, still
    I'm living with a split personality,
    Life is very complex you'll agree.
    Sometimes my mother's dominant
    And I behave so well,
    Then Father sees his chance, and
    Good intentions go to . . .
    Somewhere very hot!
    While I'm left standing in the middle,
    Trying neither to offend,
    For I'm living with a split personality
    And no-one knows who'll triumph in the end!
    I hope it's Father,
    I know I'd rather.
    I'll stand the bother
    If he'll stand the pace!
    For faced with this kind of split personality
    You bet that Father triumphs in the end!

Wedding bells signal the entrance of the ensemble

Villagers enter, followed by Mme Blum, Tony, Prudence, Mrs Lukyn, William, Jeremiah, Phoebe and finally Mathilde and Charteris. William has a tray with glasses, a jug of water, and wine, which he sets down

Everyone takes a glass and sings

No. 7 Finaletto (Act I, Scene 1)

Villagers
It's the wedding day
  Of the happy pair;
Why they ran away
  Isn't our affair.
Wish them now they're wed,
  Happiness and wealth;
As they've kindly said
  We may drink their health!

Mathilde
It's our wedding day,
We're a happy pair;
Feasting let us stay
In the open air,
Where the branches old
  In the roof combine,
And the sun—the sun is gold
  In the golden wine!
The golden wine!

Charteris
A toast to my lady wife,
  For she is of high degree,
But she has given her heart and life,
  For love alone to me,
A health to the bride!

Villagers A health to the bride!

Tony (*offering a glass to Prudence; quoting from FitzGerald's "Omar Khayyám"*) "... beneath the bough, A Flask of Wine, a Book of Verse—and Thou" ...

Prudence Nay, friend, it were forbidden "to look upon the wine".

Tony Would they forbid thee all the joys of life?

Prudence (*sighing*) It seemeth so—there can be little wickedness in just one taste ...

Tony Would I ask you if there were?

Prudence Truly, I think not, friend Tony, but—(*she pours water from a jug into a glass and sings*)

    I'm a Quaker's daughter,
    So I drink the toast in water.

Charteris (*speaking*) Now one toast more. Let's drink to love.

Tony (*singing*) Now do, Miss Prue.
It's nice, I've tried it,
You try—it's dry,
Had ice outside it!

Jeremiah
I know you'll like it rather,
I do—and so does Father.

Prudence
Thy wine on me is wasted,
Such things I never tasted.

Act I, Scene 1   19

Tony	Just one, there's nothing in it!
Tutti	Just one, you must begin it!
	She will drink it, we'll be bound,
	To love—that makes the world, the world go round!
Prudence	Thee asks me, so I'll agree,
	Tho' thee is a sad mischief-maker,
	Talking of wine and of love to me—
	That is not the way of a Quaker.

(*Raising her glass; speaking*) To Love! (*She sings*)

                Love, though I never have met you,
                Love, that I never may meet,
                Those who have known you and knelt at your throne,
                Say you are cruel and sweet!
                Some would be glad to forget you—
                You are so sad to recall,
                Ah, be what you will,
                You may come to me still,
                Love, you are lord of us all!

Tutti	Love, you're the brightest of bubbles,
	Out of the gold of the wine.
	Love, you're the gleam
	Of a wonderful dream,
	Foolish and sweet and divine!
	Yet, tho' the most of our troubles
	Come when we answer your call,
	Oh, all of us bow,
	As we drink to you now—
	Love, you are lord of us all!
	Love you are lord,
	Love you are lord of us all,
	Of us all!

Nathaniel, Rachel and the full chorus of Quakers enter and sing

Nathaniel, Rachel and Quakers	(*to Prudence*) What is thee doing here?
	Come with us for we command it.
Jeremiah	No she won't, never fear!
	Stop your talk we will not stand it
Nathaniel, Rachel and Quakers	Come away, reckless maid!
	Do not sit among the scoffers.
Jeremiah	You need not be afraid,
	Take the chance of fun that offers!
Nathaniel, Rachel and Quakers	Leave them all upon the spot!
	Or we say we know thee not!
	Or we say we know thee not!
Mme Blum	Sapristi, let them be!
	Come with me, to Paree!

Mathilde	(*to Prudence*) Come with us! Come to Paree!
	Ah, Paree!
	That is the place to see,
	For love and song and life and light,
	And laughter all the day and night.
	Ah, Paree!
	Merry and gay and free!
	The flower of earth, the mother of mirth!
	Paree, Paree, Paree!
All except Quakers	Ah, Paree,
	That is the place to see,
	For love and song and life and light,
	And laughter all the day and night
	Ah, Paree,
	Merry and gay and free!
	The flower of earth, the mother of mirth!
	Paree, Paree, Paree!
Quakers	Thee has chosen, it's the end;
	Thee is now no more a Friend,
	Go with those that laugh and play,
	Till they lead thy feet astray!
	Thee may laugh and jest and scoff
	That today we cast thee off,
	Thee will see the end and know—
	Finding no repentance—go!
Mathilde	⎧ Come, my dear
	⎪ It isn't worth a tear
	⎪ For if the old life's done
	⎪ The new is begun.
	⎪ So forget,
	⎪ You will be happy yet.
	⎪ There is another world for you to know,
	⎪ Say goodbye and let them go!
Others	⎨ She has chosen, it's the end;
	⎪ She is now no more a Friend,
	⎪ But maybe she'll find today
	⎪ She has kinder friends than they.
	⎪ Though she'd rather weep than scoff
	⎪ When her people send her off,
	⎪ She may find it better, so
	⎪ Say goodbye and let them go!
Quakers	⎪ Thee has chosen, it's the end;
	⎪ Thee is now no more a Friend,
	⎪ Go with those that laugh and play,
	⎪ Till they lead thy feet astray!
	⎪ Thee may laugh and jest and scoff
	⎪ That today we cast thee off,
	⎪ Thee will see the end and know—
	⎩ Finding no repentance—go!

Act I, Scene 2

Prudence	You bid me go?
Mathilde and Others	{ She shall go!
Quakers	{ She must go!
Prudence	You bid me go?
Mathilde and Others	{ She shall go!
Quakers	{ She must go!
Prudence	Whatever life may give
	At least, at least I'll live.
	Love, with whatever comes after,
	Gaily I answer your call.
All except Quakers	So do what you will,
	We will follow you still—
	Love, you are lord of us all.
	Ah, Paree!
	That is the place to see,
	For love and song and life and light,
	And laughter all the day and night.
	Ah, Paree,
	Merry and gay and free!
	The flower of earth, the mother of mirth!
	Paree, Paree, Paree!

The frontcloth comes in

SCENE 2

On the way to Paris (frontcloth). Immediately following

Mathilde, Phoebe, Prudence, Mme Blum, Tony, Charteris and Jeremiah enter and sing

No. 8 A Runaway Match

Mathilde	If this was two hundred years ago,
	In days of powder and patch,
	We two would have fallen in love I know,
	And struck up a runaway match!
Mathilde and Charteris	A runaway, runaway match!
Charteris	I'd call for you at the postern door
	Discreetly left on the latch,
	Then Gretna Green in a coach and four,
	And ho, for a runaway match!

Both	A runaway, runaway match,
	A runaway, runaway match for us,
	Of the good old galloping kind,
	When a guardian armed with a blunderbuss
	Is following close behind!
	And all in a fury and fume and fuss
	The couple he'd try and catch,
	By firing his gun away
	After the runaway,
	Runaway, runaway match!
Phoebe	Then I'd be your faithful lady's maid,
	A bundle of gowns I'd snatch,
	Including a hoop and a white brocade
	To wear at the runaway match.
All	The runaway, runaway match!
Tony	I'd drive the coach over ruts and rocks,
	In a wig that's known as a scratch,
	I'd look very striking on the box
	In the light of a runaway match!
	A runaway, runaway match!
All	A runaway, runaway match of old,
	When the horses tremble and pant;
	And we're always told that the coachman bold
	Must marry the confidant!
	One wedding'll make many more we're told,
	And all be wed in a batch,
	If law hadn't done away
	Now with the runaway,
	Runaway, runaway match!
Mathilde	A runaway, runaway match of old,
Mme Blum	When the horses tremble and pant;
Phoebe	And we're always told that the coachman bold
Prudence	Must marry the confidant!
	One wedding'll make many more we're told,
	And all be wed in a batch,
	If law hadn't done away
	Now with the runaway,
	Runaway, runaway match!
All	A runaway, runaway match of old,
	When the horses tremble and pant;
	And we're always told that the coachman bold
	Must marry the confidant!
	One wedding'll make many more we're told,
	And all be wed in a batch,
	If law hadn't done away
	Now with the runaway,
	Runaway, runaway, runaway,

Act I, Scene 3

        Runaway, runaway, runaway,
        Runaway match!

The frontcloth is flown out

Scene 3

La Maison Blum, a Parisian fashion house. A few weeks later

No. 9   Shop Ballet

Toinette, Shop Girls and Lady Customers are involved in the "Shop Ballet". When it finishes, the Lady Customers crowd round Toinette, making lots of noise

1st Lady ⎫   ⎧ When can I have my Quaker dress?
2nd Lady ⎬ (*together*) ⎨ When is Mme Blum going to hold a show?
3rd Lady ⎭   ⎩ When will they be ready? (*Etc.*)
Toinette I am sorry, mesdames, but you must speak personally to Mme Blum.

Mme Blum enters

Mme Blum Bonjour, mesdames!
1st Lady ⎫   ⎧ Dear Mme Blum, you promised me!
2nd Lady ⎬ (*together*) ⎨ I simply must be the first!
3rd Lady ⎭   ⎩ When will it be ready?
Mme Blum Mesdames, mesdames! I am mortified, but I cannot yet reveal the Quakaire collection. It is not yet finished, but in a few days perhaps, ha? (*She starts to show them out*) I promise you, mesdames, you will be the first to be costumed—Blum gives you her word.
1st Lady ⎫   ⎧ Oh many thanks, madame!
2nd Lady ⎬ (*together*) ⎨ Dear Madame Blum!
3rd Lady ⎭   ⎩ So very good of you!

The Lady Customers exit

Mme Blum Oh, this Quakaire mode will be the death of me. (*To the Shop Girls*) You too are tired, oui? Then take un petit quart d'heure—fifteen minutes only. And then back to work, mes enfants.
Shop Girls Oh yes, madame. Certainly, Mme Blum. Thank you.

The Shop Girls exit

Toinette stays. Mme Blum has a look through her mail

Mme Blum (*reading*) "I will try on my new costume today—Diane." Toinette!
Toinette Oui, madame?

Mme Blum Mamselle Diane, the distinguished actress comes to try on today.
Toinette Yes, madame.
Mme Blum Miss Prudence has not yet returned?
Toinette Not yet, madame.
Mme Blum I wonder how many heads she will turn today. She is a good girl, that one, Toinette.
Toinette Oh truly, madame. And if I may say so, madame, it was very clever of you to think of sending her out each day, dressed in her Quaker costume. Now the whole of Paris is talking of the Blum collection, before it has been seen; before it is even finished.
Mme Blum Ah well, Toinette, to succeed you must always be the one step ahead of everyone else.

Liane, one of the Shop Girls, enters

What is it, Liane?
Liane Madame, Monsieur Larose is here.
Mme Blum Monsieur Larose!
Toinette (*remembering*) Oh la! The Chief of Police. He has been waiting for half an hour!
Mme Blum Go then, Toinette. Go and warn the princess not to come downstairs.

Toinette exits

Liane, please show Monsieur Larose in.

Liane exits and, immediately, Larose limps in

Larose I trust, madame, it is convenient to receive me?
Mme Blum Monsieur, one is always enchanté to receive the honour of a visit from the police.
Larose Madame has recently journeyed to England?
Mme Blum And as monsieur may see, I have also returned.
Larose But perhaps madame did not return from England—alone?
Mme Blum Perhaps monsieur would care to explain?
Larose Certainly. Our information is that madame was accompanied by a young lady.
Mme Blum Ah, monsieur must be referring to——
Larose I do not mean the charming Quaker Girl who has created such a great sensation in Paris, but (*impressively*) the Princess Mathilde—exiled and forbidden ever to return to France.
Mme Blum (*feigning outrage*) Monsieur!
Larose (*impassively*) Madame! The Princess Mathilde was married in England to a Captain Charteris. Unfortunately, they were imprudent enough to return to France to spend a brief honeymoon at Barbizon.
Mme Blum And I, monsieur? What has this to do with me?
Larose You shall hear, madame. After a honeymoon of three days at Barbizon, Captain Charteris is sent on one of his official journeys to

Act I, Scene 3   25

Madrid. The cottage at Barbizon is closed, the princess disappears—where to? That we do not know.
Mme Blum Eh voilà! That is surely the end of the story?
Larose Not so. It is perhaps madame who can finish it. I ask *you*, where is the Princess Mathilde?
Mme Blum And if I say I do not know, monsieur?
Larose Then the story ends, perhaps, unhappily for you, madame.

No. 10   The Name That You'll Remember

Mme Blum
  (*singing*)   You can't believe that I'd deceive
                Our Chief of Police;
                That bastion of law,
                Defender of peace,
                Student of the criminal mind,
                Police technique that's so refined,
                Master of disguise and so much more!
                For while the famous men to come
                Will have their day and then be gone,
                Larose is the name that you'll remember!

Larose (*speaking*) A police search at La Maison Blum would be a most regrettable incident.
Mme Blum Monsieur, surely you are not insinuating . . . ?
Larose Oh madame, I insinuate nothing—I merely ask for your assistance. In consideration of our friendship, madame, I am at the moment conducting this enquiry personally—and alone.
Mme Blum Monsieur honours me.
Larose Madame!

  (*Singing*)   I can be charming!
Mme Blum   You can be tough!
Larose   Some find me helpful!
Mme Blum   And others rough!
Larose   But each approach can sometimes pay,
                I use them all to get my way,
                For I'm Larose of the Sûreté
Mme Blum   And *that* is the name that you'll remember.

Larose (*speaking*) I await madame's reply.
Mme Blum I regret, monsieur, that I know nothing.
Larose (*becoming impatient*) Madame, this is the second time you have defied the law. First you smuggle the princess into France, although with no unpleasant result. But this time . . .

  (*Singing*)   I want the princess!
Mme Blum   I said she isn't here.

Larose I'm still not certain,
Mme Blum Oh!
Larose But never fear,
I'll find a way to seek her out
And when I do there'll be no doubt
Larose is the name that she'll remember!

(*Speaking*) This could mean arrest, madame!
Mme Blum Monsieur?
Larose As madame wishes. A search could destroy the reputation of Maison Blum, but ... au revoir, madame. (*He starts to go*)

Mme Blum
(*singing*) I hope you find her.
Larose Oh I will!
Mme Blum I'd like to help.
Larose You may do still.
And Larose is the name that you'll remember!

Larose exits

Mme Blum Oh but this is terrible.

Mathilde enters

Mathilde May I come down?
Mme Blum No! No! We must take great care. It is imperative that you remain hidden away at all times. The Chief of Police has been here asking about you.
Mathilde (*holding up a letter*) Never mind, Blum dear—my husband is coming back today.
Mme Blum Today? But he must not come here! We will all be ruined. Please, you must return to your room.
Mathilde Very well. Where is Prudence?
Mme Blum She is not yet returned from her promenade.
Mathilde And no sign of Mr Chute today? He does seem to come here a good deal.
Mme Blum Ah, Mr Chute. A good boy that—I do not fear him for the little Quaker girl. But if she should meet with Prince Carlo ...
Mathilde The Prince Carlo they wanted me to marry?
Mme Blum The same. If she should meet him, then we must take care to warn her of his reputation. We would not like to see her come to harm in Paris. Oh, but please you must go back to your room.
Mathilde If I must. (*She starts to go*) The bird is going to its cage again, (*holding up the letter*) but with a little piece of sugar.

Mathilde exits. Phoebe enters

Mme Blum Oh these children! Ah, Phoebe. Tell me, did anyone follow you?
Phoebe Did anyone follow me? I should think they did, madame. Why, if a girl's lonely in Paris, it's her own fault!

Mme Blum We must take care, Phoebe. The Chief of Police has been here looking for your mistress.
Phoebe Why, whatever for?
Mme Blum They would send her out of France again. Inspector Larose is a clever man, but I am also no fool.
Phoebe If he comes here, how shall I know him?
Mme Blum The Chief of Police walks so. (*She limps a few paces*)
Phoebe Limps?
Mme Blum Limps! With one leg—so! Phoebe, look out for the man who limps with one leg—so.

Mme Blum exits limping

Phoebe Hmph! If he comes around here again, I'll make him limp with two!

Jeremiah enters. He is dressed outrageously in the Paris style

Oh, so you're here at last.
Jeremiah Bonjour, Phoebe. How do you like the new get-up?
Phoebe What *are* you supposed to be?
Jeremiah Well, I'm not quite sure. Mme Blum says I'm to walk about with savoir flair.
Phoebe Well, while you're doing that, you just keep your eyes open for a man who limps—with one leg, so! (*She limps a few paces*)
Jeremiah Limps?
Phoebe Yes! The Chief of Police, and if he finds the princess, she'll be turned out of France right away, me too, I suppose.
Jeremiah Don't worry about that, you're both quite safe—I'm here to protect you. Say, Phoebe, I bought you a little present. (*He produces a fancy garter and shyly hands it to her*)
Phoebe (*without a clue what it is*) Oh, why thank you, Jerry, it's very nice I'm sure, but ... er—er ... what is it?
Jeremiah What is it? Well you see, Phoebe ... er—er ...

Toinette and the Shop Girls enter

Toinette Bonjour, Mamselle Phoebe, Monsieur Jerry.
Jeremiah }
Phoebe } (*together*) Bonjour, Toinette.
Phoebe Well, Jerry?
Jeremiah (*embarrassed*) Er ... I think I ought to go and see whether there's any sign of Prudence. (*Going rapidly*) I'll see you later.

Jeremiah exits

Phoebe But, Jerry ... ! Well, there's a fine thing.
Toinette Something is troubling mamselle?
Phoebe Well, Jerry's just given me the loveliest present, but I'm sure I can't figure out what it is.
Toinette Oh, but Mamselle Phoebe, it is very simple, eh girls?

Toinette and the Girls show a garter

Phoebe Well, I never!
Toinette Then perhaps, mamselle, you should! Please?
Phoebe Oh, I couldn't possibly! Well perhaps just for a moment. (*She goes to the mirror and puts the garter on*) This Paris air is altogether too much for Jerry. (*Admiring the garter in the mirror*) And if I stop here and wear these kind of things, it'll be too much for me! (*She sings*)

No. 11 Ah Oui

When I came over to Paris,
It was such a curious change,
Everything seemed to be different
And I felt so very strange.
People kept talking and chattering so,
What they were saying I never could know,
French is a language that bothers your brain
Again and again!
But soon I found out, though it may seem absurd,
I could answer all questions with one little word!

"Ah oui" was all that I had to say,
I soon found out the way.
So I merely said "oui, monsieur" with a bow you see,
It's a nice little word "ah oui".

Till I came over to Paris,
I had never been afloat,
So I was quite interested
When I went on board the boat.
When we set out it was pleasant enough,
But halfway across it began to get rough,
There I was holding my poor little head,
I wished I was dead!
Then a Frenchman who noticed me sitting so still,
Said "Pardon, mamselle, do you feel at all ill?"

"Ah oui" was all that I had to say,
It seemed the shortest way.
So I merely said "oui, monsieur; it's the dreadful sea,
I want to go home—ah, oui."

Phoebe, Toinette and the Shop Girls exit. Tony enters with Diane

Diane There's absolutely no use denying it, Tony, I saw you!
Tony You saw what?
Diane I saw you speak to her.
Tony So, I spoke to her. Bring back the guillotine!
Diane Not only you, but every man in Paris. Did you see them around this "Quaker Girl" at the Place de l'Opéra?

Act I, Scene 3   29

Tony You couldn't push a knife through the crowd!
Diane All of them! Prince Carlo, who fought two duels on my account—Monsieur Duhamel, the minister—all those who swore devotion to me around *her*!
Tony (*distracted*) Not at all, Diane. Have I been able to leave your side for a moment?
Diane You! Do you think I can't see that this Quaker Girl has caught you too?
Tony (*aside*) If she runs into Prudence, it'll be au revoir Tony. (*Aloud*) Say, Diane, why don't we go and buy you that lovely necklace we saw in the rue de la Paix?
Diane I don't want your presents, your necklace. It's revenge I want, revenge. Oh this Quaker Girl, I could . . .

She pushes over a tailor's dummy with her parasol. Tony catches it

Tony (*to the dummy*) Did she fall, or was she pushed!

Toinette enters

Toinette Ah, Mamselle Diane, you have come for your fitting?
Diane Yes, Toinette.
Toinette Mme Blum is just making the final adjustments. If you would please come through into the salon?
Diane Thank you, Toinette. Tony, darling, I'd like your opinion.
Tony Oh, I rather thought I'd stroll down to Rumplemayer's for coffee.
Diane The only place you're strolling, my dear, is into the salon with me. After you—darling.
Tony Charmed I'm sure.

Tony exits followed by Diane and Toinette. Jeremiah enters

Jeremiah No sign of Prudence yet. I wonder if Phoebe's managed to work out what the gift is yet. (*He sniggers*) I hope she doesn't find out how I came by it though. Oh, what a night last night was. Wouldn't Father have enjoyed it. (*He does a brief can-can step, singing a few la-la's*)

Larose enters, disguised as a wild Bohemian of Montmartre—extravagant and effusive in manner

Larose (*theatrically*) Ah! Le cher Anglais!
Jeremiah Eh? Share who?
Larose You remember—last night—ha ha! Viveur! Viveur!
Jeremiah Yes, I remember last night, but I don't remember you.
Larose Oh surely, monsieur. Montmartre. The *Café du Chat-Noir*, Les Girls?
Jeremiah (*alarmed*) Shhhh! Don't speak so loud. But how do *you* know?
Larose Ah, did I not bring you home? Did I not find the keyhole for you? Did you not make me promise to come and see you today? Ah mon ami, we will have another night of it tonight, eh? Vive le vin! Vive les femmes! Vive l'amour!
Jeremiah Righto! Fever! Fever!

Larose starts to sing and dance the can-can. Jeremiah joining in
  Phoebe enters, and points out Larose's limp to Jeremiah
Larose continues, oblivious of her presence
  (*Seeing her*) Phoebe!
Phoebe (*in a stage whisper*) The man with the limp. The Chief of Police!
Larose turns and sees Phoebe
Larose Mamselle, enchanté!
Phoebe (*very broad country dialect*) Be this gentleman a friend of yours, Jerry?
Larose Ah oui, mamselle, we are camarades, Monsieur Jerry and I. I meet him last night, and he tells me of a charming princess here.
Phoebe A princess? (*Simpering*) Monsewer flatters me, I'm sure.
Jeremiah I'm afraid there's no princess here, (*bustling him out*) and you mustn't be caught here either.
Phoebe It would be more than our place was worth.
Jeremiah Mme Blum would sack us toot sweet.
Larose Ah, monsieur, mamselle, may I propose a little refreshment?
Jeremiah (*still bustling him out*) Yes, that's it, you go and wait for us.
Larose At the café at the corner of the street?
Jeremiah Yes, that's it.
Larose You won't be long?
Jeremiah No, we won't be long, eh Phoebe?
Phoebe No, we won't be long.
Larose The café at the corner!

  Larose exits

Jeremiah (*shouting after him*) Mind you wait for us!
Phoebe (*shouting*) We shan't be more than a day or two!
Phoebe
Jeremiah } (*together*) Phew! (*They shake hands*)
Jeremiah Well done, partner. Fever indeed!
Phoebe We'd best tell Mme Blum. Jerry, you go and find her. I'll keep an eye out in case he comes back.

Jeremiah starts to go

  Jerry, what did he mean by fever?
Jeremiah I dunno—running a temperature I expect.

  Jeremiah exits

Phoebe occupies herself with some trivial task
  Charteris enters

Charteris Hello, Phoebe.
Phoebe Oh, sir, you're back.
Charteris Where's Mathilde? I must see her.

Act I, Scene 3

Tony enters, cautiously looking back

Tony Phoebe, have you seen Miss Prudence? (*Seeing Charteris*) Charteris!
Charteris Hello, Chute old man. Where is she?
Tony (*pointing to where he has just come from*) She's in there.
Charteris Then excuse me, I've spent far too long away from my wife already.
Tony Your wife? No, I mean Diane!
Charteris Diane. Oh is that still on?
Tony As far as she's concerned it is. She worships the very ground—that's coming to me!
Charteris Phoebe, go and tell your mistress I'm here—no, tell me where she is, and I'll go to her.
Phoebe Which shall I do first?

Mme Blum enters

Charteris Ah, Mme Blum!
Mme Blum Monsieur, you must not be seen here. Go! Go!
Charteris But I've come for my wife.
Mme Blum Monsieur, you cannot have her! The police!
Charteris Mme Blum, don't worry. I'll take good care of her. Now I'm sorry, but I can't wait a moment longer. (*Going*) It's this way I presume?
Mme Blum No! No! Monsieur, these are the apartments of my girls. Oh mon Dieu! Phoebe, please show Captain Charteris to Mathilde's room vite!

Phoebe and Captain Charteris exit

Monsieur Tony, Madame Diane asks for you là.
Tony (*shaking his head, starting to go*) "Once more into the breach, dear friends ..." (*To a dummy close by the exit*) Are you any good with a sword? You are? Come with me!

Tony takes the dummy off with him

Mme Blum Oh these children!

There are noises off

Prudence enters, surrounded by admiring gentlemen Newspaper Reporters

Reporters (*together*) { Oh please, Miss Pym, say you'll have dinner with me.
I simply have to see you again.
How long are you going to be in Paris? (*Etc.*)
Mme Blum Please, please! Gentlemen, gentlemen!
Prudence Oh, it's all right, Mme Blum, these gentlemen have been kind enough to escort me back here.
1st Reporter Mme Blum, could I just have a few words from you for my newspaper? The whole of Paris wants to know what the Blum Quaker Collection will look like.
2nd Reporter Oh, yes, just a few words, Mme Blum.

Mme Blum Messieurs, there is much work to be done before the Blum Quakaire Collection can be revealed—n'est ce pas, Miss Prudence?
Prudence Oui, madame. And now gentlemen, if you will excuse me, *I* have much work to do also. Please?

They reluctantly leave

Mme Blum Ah, Miss Prudence, you must be careful not to fatigue yourself too much. This admiration is all very well, but . . .
Prudence Oh dear Mme Blum, I am enjoying myself so much. Paris is beautiful and everyone is so nice to me. And I have such exciting news. This morning I met a prince!
Mme Blum Aha! The Prince Carlo, n'est ce pas?
Prudence Why, yes, but——
Mme Blum Ah bien! But accept the word of advice and take care with him.
Prudence (*laughing*) He has been taking care of me all morning. Oh what would Aunt Rachel say?
Mme Blum She would also tell you to take care! It was to the Prince Carlo they would have married our Mathilde.
Prudence Oh, and now he talks as though he wanted to marry me.
Mme Blum To *marry* you? No, no, that is not his way.
Prudence No matter. I will do as you say, and take care. But, madame, we are all invited to the prince's enclosure at Chantilly Races next week.
Mme Blum We? All?
Prudence Why yes. When at first I refused, telling him that I would be *too* busy helping with the final touches to your collection, he insisted that the entire staff of Maison Blum must take a rest and join him at the Races.
Mme Blum (*an idea*) Ah! The inspiration! The prince's private enclosure at the most fashionable racecourse in France. C'est parfait, n'est ce pas?
Prudence I don't understand.
Mme Blum Miss Prudence, we *shall* go to the races, and there we shall reveal—the Blum Quakaire Collection!
Prudence Oh Mme Blum, what a wonderful idea! I can hardly wait.
Mme Blum Now, we must find somewhere very quiet for a few days where we can work without the interruption. Ah, I have it. My brother he has a little cottage at Barbizon. C'est parfait, n'est ce pas?
Prudence C'est parfait, Mme Blum.

They embrace excitedly

Charteris and Mathilde enter

Mme Blum Monsieur! I repeat, it is impossible for you to be here.
Charteris Ah, but you see, I am here!
Mathilde And we're never going to part again, are we?
Charteris Never!

Phoebe enters

Phoebe Shall I pack the grey hat, madame?
Mathilde Yes, please, Phoebe.

Act I, Scene 3   33

Phoebe exits

Mme Blum The grey hat? Where are you going?
Charteris We're going back to Barbizon to finish our honeymoon.
Mme Blum But it's impossible. The police watch Barbizon.
Charteris (*good-naturedly*) Mme Blum sees the police at every turn.
Mme Blum I tell you, they would send my darling out of France!
Charteris Ha, ha! Let them try.
Mme Blum Oh, if I could only tell you in English what I think of you in French. Very well. At least, if I am also at Barbizon, I can keep an eye on you both. Oh these children!

Jeremiah enters

Mathilde You in Barbizon?
Mme Blum Oui. I will explain later—but now there is much to do.
Prudence Mme Blum. Would you excuse me. I should like to leave a note for Tony—I mean Mr Chute.
Mme Blum Oh, very well, but vite ha? We must lose no time.

Prudence exits

Phoebe enters

Phoebe Everything is packed, madame.
Jeremiah Where are you going, Phoebe?
Phoebe To Barbizon!
Jeremiah To Barbizon?
All To Barbizon!

No. 12   Barbizon

Mathilde	Away together
	In lovers' weather,
	To have our joyous June
	Honeymoon!
Charteris	In forest alleys
	And grassy valleys
	We'll lead the simple life,
	Little wife!
Jeremiah	I shall be chuckling
	To feed a duckling
Phoebe	And meet a tree that's not
	In a pot.
Mme Blum	I'll have my ration
	Of rustic fashion
	And be quite à la mode
	In the wode.
All	Oh, it feels so good
	When you wander in the wood.
	Away to balmy Barbizon!
	For such a happy time we'll go,

	And have a cottage where our chanticleer
	At three a.m. will crow!
	Away in balmy Barbizon
	The breezes play a gay chanson,
	And little lambs afar,
	Will echo ev'ry bar
	In balmy—Barbizon!
Mathilde	It will be pleasant
	To play a peasant,
Charteris	And live on curds and cream—
	What a dream!
Phoebe	I'll look my smartest,
	To catch an artist,
	I'll show him if I ain't
	Fit to paint!
Jeremiah	I'll take my chances
	At village dances,
	And do dare-devil things
	On the swings!
Mme Blum	I'll cut a figure
	Of rustic vigour,
	And dress with perfect taste—
	What a waste!
All	Oh, we'll laugh all day,
	As we tumble in the hay.
	Away to balmy Barbizon!
	For such a happy time we'll go,
	And have a cottage where our chanticleer
	At three a.m. will crow.
	Away in balmy Barbizon,
	The breezes play a gay chanson,
	And little lambs afar
	Will echo ev'ry bar
	In balmy Barbizon!

The Shop Girls enter and perform a dance sequence

> And little lambs afar
>   Will echo ev'ry bar
> In balmy Barbi, balmy Barbi,
>   Balmy Barbizon!

Everyone exits

Act I, Scene 3   35

No. 12A   Act I Finale

Music underscores the following

Diane enters, followed by Tony

Diane You know, Tony, I think that necklace in the rue de la Paix will go splendidly with my new dress after all, don't you agree?
Tony (*distractedly*) Yes, I expect it will.

Prudence enters with a note

Prudence Tony!
Tony Hello, Prudence.
Diane Good-day, *Miss Pym*.
Prudence Mme Lefevre.
Diane Well, Tony, are you going to buy me that *gorgeous necklace* or aren't you?
Tony I . . . er . . .
Diane *Well, darling?*
Tony (*sensing a row, and wanting to avoid it*) If you'll excuse me, I'll be back shortly. *Please* don't go away.

Tony and Diane exit

Prudence, dejected, looks off the way he has gone, then down at the note she has written to him. She tears it up, drops it on the floor, and retires slowly upstage, as——

— the CURTAIN *falls*

ACT II

Scene 1

Prince Carlo's private enclosure at Chantilly Racecourse. The following week

The Curtain *rises on Prince Carlo, Mme Blum, Diane, M. Duhamel, Minister of State, and various Guests. They sing*

No. 13 Opening Chorus "At Chantilly" and Mannequin Parade

All	Here we are at Chantilly,
	Watching all the races
	We have won, as you can see
	By our happy faces!
	Here we are at Chantilly!
	All of us are winners:
Ladies	There'll be gloves for us, maybe,
	Gowns and little dinners!
All	Here we are at Chantilly,
	Watching all the races,
	We have won, as you can see
	By our happy faces!
Men	We're here at the races,
	With pockets and cases
	All bursting with paper of heavenly blue!
	We love a love letter,
	But these are far better,
	The billet de banque is the true billet-doux,
	The true billet-doux!
	And it's all thro' the luck of our mascot and maiden,
	Our hearts are so light and our purses so laden,
	The layer, the backer, the wily bookmaker,
	They're left at the post by the dear little Quaker!
All	The layer, the backer, the wily bookmaker,
	They're left at the post by the dear little Quaker!
	The dear little, queer little Quaker!

Mannequins enter dressed in the Quaker collection, Prudence last of all

That's the style you have to copy,
   That's the dress the men will love!
Not the scarlet of the poppy,
   But the plumage of the dove!

Act II, Scene 1   37

>   Quakerism's our religion,
>   So if men should come to woo,
>   Like the modest little pigeon,
>   We would simply answer, coo!
>   We would simply answer coo!

At the end, the Company applaud Mme Blum and Prince Carlo approaches her

Prince Congratulations, madame. As usual, a new Blum Collection creates a sensation.
Mme Blum Your highness is most gracious.
Prince (*turning to Prudence*) And, mamselle, you have Paris at your feet — and Paris is not easily conquered.
Prudence Thank you. I am enjoying myself so much. And I am so pleased that your beautiful horse won. It was very lucky.
Prince It was indeed. You kissed it in the paddock!
Prudence (*in her defensive Quaker style*) Thou art very kind, friend.
Prince Then this is your first visit to Paris, mamselle?
Prudence Oh yes, I have never been away from my village in England.
Prince It must now be desolate. You will allow me, I hope, to do what I can to make your stay here a pleasant one?
Prudence You are very kind, monsieur, but I must not let your kindness make me forget that I am after all, only a mannequin of La Maison Blum.
Prince That, dear Miss Prudence, is easily altered.
Prudence I don't understand, monsieur.
Prince Then, please give me an opportunity to explain later. But now, mamselle, I have a favour to beg. Will you honour me by coming to my ball tonight? It will be the happiest moment of my life.
Prudence Ball? Oh, but I've never been to a ball, monsieur.
Prince Then you must allow me the pleasure of enjoying your first impressions.
Lady Guest (*coming forward*) Prince Carlo. They want to hear the story of Mimi; may I tell it?
Prince Madame, I place my reputation at your disposal.
Mme Blum (*coming forward*) No! No stories of the prince in front of my girls.
Lady Guest Oh this one is not shocking — only amusing.
Mme Blum Then it cannot be true.

The Prince retires upstage to a group of ladies

Duhamel (*approaching Prudence*) Mamselle, let me give you a little advice. Beware of the prince. These little suppers and dances are called "His Highness's Mousetraps".
Prudence Mousetraps? Why thank you, Monsieur Duhamel. I promise that if I go to the ball, I will be very careful.
Duhamel And if I can be of *any* service to you, please remember, it will be a pleasure. (*He retires upstage*)

Prince Carlo comes downstage

Prince Mamselle, let me give you a little advice—Monsieur Duhamel is still ... dangerous.
Prudence That is most kind of you both.
Prince Both?
2nd Lady Guest Prince, do help us to pick the next winner!

The Prince retires to another group of ladies

During the following, Charteris and Mathilde enter but stay tucked away

Prudence (*to Mme Blum*) Why do they call this ball "The Mousetrap", madame?
Mme Blum Because it is set for you. You are the mouse. Le souris.
Prudence Souris? But souris is also French for smile is it not, madame?
Mme Blum Sometimes.
Prudence (*laughing*) Then the mouse can smile at the trap.
Mathilde Psst!

Mme Blum looks around her, then sees them

Mme Blum (*rushing to them, horrified*) Are you mad? What are you doing here in the prince's enclosure? If he sees you, all is lost.
Mathilde Oh, dear Blum, we couldn't possibly let your new collection be revealed without being here. It's a great success.
Charteris I promise, madame, we shall be discretion itself. There are so many people here, we'll hardly be noticed.
Mme Blum Then for a short time only, hein? But please, you must take care. I have an idea. In the ladies' marquee, là, you will find a spare Quakaire costume. Go put it on. Then it will appear that you are one of my mannequins.
Mathilde Dear Blum—still so cautious. Very well, I will do as you say.

Charteris and Mathilde exit

Mme Blum Oh these children!
Prince (*coming downstage*) Mesdames, messieurs! I give you a ball this evening at the *Pré-Catalan*—will you all give me the pleasure of your company?

General murmur of thanks and polite applause

(*To Mme Blum*) And I hope, madame, that you will allow your young ladies to come also.
Mme Blum And I, monsieur? What about me?
Prince Oh, madame, your invitation is understood.
Mme Blum And if I come will you dance with me all the evening?
Prince (*laughing*) Madame, why am I so honoured?
Mme Blum It will keep you out of mischief.
Prince (*laughing*) Then, mesdames, messieurs, this evening at the ball. (*He sings*)

Act II, Scene 1

No. 14 Come to the Ball

Come with me, come to the ball
   Music and merriment call.
Golden and gay are the lamps above
   Every tune is a song of love!
Ladies that come to the ball,
   I am in love with you all.
Each has a part of my heart
   At the ball! At the ball!
Come to the dances,
   Come while you may,
Flow'rs and romances
   Fade with the day;
Come in your beauty,
   Fair as a rose,
Dancing's a duty
   Ev'ryone owes!
Leave me not lonely,
   When I implore,
You are the only
   Girls I adore!
I will be loyal,
   True to you all,
Hailing you royal
   Queens of the ball.

Chorus Hailing us Queens of the ball!
Prince Say, will you come to the ball?
   Who will not answer the call?
Join in the maze of the waltz that whirls,
   Gallant young lovers and laughing girls,
All of you come to the ball,
   There will be welcome for all,
Chance for a dance,
   And romance,
At the ball—at the ball!

Chorus Gladly we'll come to the ball,
   None but will answer the call,
All of us long for the waltz that whirls,
   Gallant young lovers and laughing girls.
All of you (Ah, let us) come to the ball,
   There will be joy (welcome) for us all,
Chance for a dance
   And romance,
At the ball— at the ball.
   Chance for a dance
And romance,
   At the ball—at the ball.

Everyone exits leaving Prince Carlo and Diane alone

Diane approaches the Prince

Prince Ah, Diane! More charming than ever.
Diane Your Highness.
Prince I hope that you too will accept my invitation to a little supper and dance this evening?
Diane Is the Quaker Girl to be there?
Prince I hope so.
Diane Then, thank you, I will.
Prince Diane, I understand that Mr Chute pays more than a little attention to Mamselle Prudence. It would please me more if he was not so much in evidence ... ?
Diane I am happy to inform his Highness that Mr Chute and Miss Pym have not now seen each other for a week. I will see to it that that situation continues. It so happens that I have with me some of his more amorous letters to me, just in case they should prove to be ... useful.
Prince Amorous ... ?
Diane (*offering them*) Judge for yourself.
Prince (*declining*) Thank you, but it is your affair. You seem to have quite a collection. Are mine there?
Diane Oh, yes, (*laughing*) yours and Monsieur Duhamel's. How Paris would laugh at our premier Minister of State in love! But these are not for the little Quaker Girl.
Prince I trust you will have the success you deserve. Now, may I escort you to the paddock? My best filly runs in the next race.

Tony enters

Diane Thank you.

Tony darts back out of sight as Diane and Prince Carlo exit and reappears when they have gone

Tony I don't know about the prince's filly, but I reckon I've run six furlongs myself today, trying to dodge Diane. And still no sign of Prudence. I've got to find her and straighten things out. (*He pours himself a drink*)

Prudence enters

Prudence How do you do, Mr Chute.
Tony Prudence, I've been looking all over for you. I haven't seen you for more than a week.
Prudence Oh, I'm afraid I've been very busy with the collection. And in any case I expect that you've been busy with Mme Lefevre's shopping.
Tony Mme Lefevre's ... ? Now listen, Prudence ... Diane and me ... why that's just a terrible misunderstanding. She's not really interested in me, nor I in her. But she's a determined lady, who doesn't know how to accept a gracious defeat.
Prudence Then you aren't in love with her?
Tony In love with Diane? Prudence, I have eyes only for one girl—when I

Act II, Scene 1   41

can see her that is! These days that's not easy— she always seems to have a crowd of admirers around her.
Prudence Yes, they are rather nice to me.
Tony Prince Carlo especially, I suppose. Do you know he's——
Prudence (*laughing*) You're going to warn me against him, I expect.
Tony Well yes ...
Prudence That's just what all the men here do about each other.
Tony Prudence, this last week, I've never stopped thinking about you.
Prudence Really?
Tony Every moment.
Prudence I thought about thee, too—once or twice.
Tony You did? You know, you make me the happiest man alive when you say that.
Prudence They say thee talks to many maidens thus, friend Tony.
Tony There are no maidens like thee to talk thus to.
Prudence Verily?
Tony Verily!
Prudence But this is Paris, and everyone says nice things to me in Paris.
Tony Let's leave Paris, and I'll say them to you somewhere else.
Prudence Oh, but I don't want to leave Paris. There's so much to see and I've been invited to a ball this evening.
Tony A ball? Say you won't go. Promise you won't dance with anyone but me.
Prudence (*smiling*) No, I cannot promise that.
Tony Why not?
Prudence Because, friend Tony, I do not know how to dance—even with thee.
Tony Really? Then I'll show you. Right here and now!

No. 15   A Dancing Lesson

Prudence (*singing*)	Will you kindly tell me what I Should do?
Tony	Well, you take a step, take a step, take a step!
Prudence	I have taken one, and now I Take two!
Tony	Take another step! Take a step, take a step!
Prudence	I'm afraid you'll find me sadly Too slow!
Tony	Only, take a step, take a step, take a step!
Prudence	I am doing very badly I know.

They polka

Tony	Now suppose that we take Up the waltz?
Prudence	I'm afraid I shall make Many faults!

Tony	Never mind the amount—
	Hold to me!
	And remember to count,
	One, two, three!
Prudence	I'll remember to count
	One, two, three.
Both (*speaking*)	One, two, three—one, two, three!
(*Singing*)	Now we'll try—
Prudence (*slipping*)	Oh, you will drop me.
Tony	
(*catching her*)	Not I!
Prudence	After a day of it,
	I'll get the way of it.
Tony	By and by.

They waltz

Prudence	I'm really learning how it's done,
	It seems to me delightful fun!
	And if it does not weary you,
	Once more we'll take it through.

They waltz

	I am sure to make a blunder
	Somehow.
Tony	Only take a step, take a step, take a step!
Prudence	Am I going right, I wonder
	Till now?
Tony	Yes, you take a step, take a step, take a step!
Prudence	You're a perfect dancing master
	For skill.
Tony	I can take a step, take a step, take a step!
Prudence	Now, I'd like to try it faster—
Both	We will.

They polka

Diane enters at the end of the dance and approaches them. She holds a bundle of letters

Diane Well, what a pretty picture. Oh don't look so alarmed, Tony. I'm not going to play the jilted lover. I prefer a role with more subtlety. I've just come to give Miss Pym a little gift.

Tony What is it?

Diane Just some letters. Some charmingly-written letters.

Tony Letters?

Diane Your letters to me. Happy reading, Miss Pym.

   Diane exits

Tony walks away embarrassed

Act II, Scene 1

Prudence You once returned something to me when I asked you not to read it. Before *you* ask, these I return to you.
Tony She knows I love you, Prudence. She knows I can think of no-one else since I met you. You do believe me? In spite of everything they may say?
Prudence In spite of everything. (*She hands back the letters*)
Tony (*looking down at them*) What's this? She's made a mistake — these aren't mine.
Prudence Not yours?
Tony No, but I recognize the writing. They are from Monsieur Duhamel, the minister. Mamselle was proposing to use these against *him* I suppose?
Prudence Oh, then I'll return them to him myself — a charming gentleman.
Tony Prudence, you won't go to Prince Carlo's ball tonight will you? It's not where I should like to see — my future wife.
Prudence Then I won't go, Tony.
Tony You promise?
Prudence I promise.
Tony May I make one more request?
Prudence What is it?
Tony (*embarrassed*) Well I ... er ... (*An idea!*) Wouldst thou allow me to kiss thee, friend Prudence?
Prudence Friend Tony, I was beginning to think that thou wouldst never ask.

They kiss and exit

Jeremiah enters, with Josephine, a mannequin, and Toinette on each arm, and followed by the others. He has a handful of money

Jeremiah Well, I must say, Father's in good form today! Every one a winner! Say, Josephine, are you doing anything particular this evening?
Josephine Monsieur Jeremiah, we are always very particular about what we do in the evening.
Jeremiah Well, how about a cosy little table d'hôte at *Le Chat Noir*? Only cost you ten francs.
Josephine What, pay for ourselves? We are going to the *Pré-Catalan* to the prince's ball.
Jeremiah (*casually*) Oh, is that tonight? I promised to look in — late. Say, girls, you'll keep me a dance, won't you?

Phoebe enters upstage

Toinette What about Mamselle Phoebe?
Jeremiah Phoebe? Oh, Phoebe's all right — of course she's a bit on the jealous side — but there's no need to tell her everything we do is there?
Phoebe (*coming forward*) Not a bit, when she can see for herself!
Jeremiah Phoebe, I was just——
Phoebe Yes, I know you were — I caught you at it!
Josephine Is the offer still open for dinner, Monsieur Jeremiah?
Phoebe Not tonight, Josephine! Now, what were you doing with your arms around those French girls, I'd like to know?

The girls move away

Jeremiah It's this place, Phoebe, and all this bubbly stuff we keep drinking. My arms are getting a permanent curve on them. Look at this one! Waiting for you, Phoebe! (*He slips his arm around her waist*)

Phoebe I don't think you've behaved at all nicely to me since we've been here.

Jeremiah I'll make up for it, as soon as we get away.

Phoebe I wish I could believe you, Jerry. This sort of thing is all very well, but a good old-fashioned game of kiss-in-the-ring on our village green takes a lot of beating.

Jeremiah Well, we're a bit above that sort of thing now, mixing with princes and princesses. You know, Phoebe, I always felt that I should get on in the world.

Phoebe So did I.

Jeremiah You see, we'll be a couple of high-society types some day! (*He sings*)

No. 16　The Season

	We are invited everywhere
	By people we can't say no to.
Phoebe	We are delighted you will be there
	For we shall be sure to go, too.
Jeremiah	We'll have a daily ride in the morn
	And let our electric car be.
Phoebe	Then we will gaily tootle the horn
	And drive to the Oaks or Derby.
Both	The Derby, the Derby,
	We'll drive to the Oaks or Derby
	Derby, Derby, Derby.
	The season, the season,
	We'll get in a set and we'll freeze on
	Never stopping, never slowing,
	Set the pace and keep it going.
	The season, the season.
	You'll be late if you wait for a reason,
	For it's fashion's whim
	To be in the swim
	At the height of the London season.

The season, the season,
We'll get in a set and we'll freeze on,
Never stopping, never slowing,
Set the pace and keep it going.
The season, the season.
You'll be late if you wait for a reason
For it's fashion's whim
To be in the swim
At the heat of the London season.

Act II, Scene 1   45

Mme Blum, Charteris and Mathilde enter at the end of the song. The general company start to enter, including Duhamel

Mme Blum And now chérie, you will make Blum's heart beat steadier if you would leave, hein?
Charteris But, Mme Blum——
Mme Blum Please, no "buts".
Mathilde Very well. But first, I must congratulate your girls—they look so splendid. (*She goes up to the group of Mannequins*)

Larose enters with two Gendarmes

Larose Monsieur Duhamel, you are in charge here?
Duhamel Well, the prince is still in the paddock, so until his return I suppose I am.
Larose Then, monsieur, I regret that I am compelled to intrude in my official capacity, bearing the warrant which you yourself signed only this morning, for the arrest and deportation from France of the Princess Mathilde. I have reason to believe that she is here at this moment.
Charteris (*stepping forward*) Monsieur, the Princess Mathilde is now my wife.
Larose Monsieur refers to his marriage in England?
Charteris Certainly.
Larose Ah, monsieur apparently does not know that such a marriage is not valid in France.
Charteris
Mme Blum } (*together*) Not valid?
Larose No, monsieur, another marriage in France is necessary to make your union legal, (*to Duhamel*) n'est ce pas, monsieur?
Duhamel I'm afraid that's the way the law stands at the moment, although ——
Charteris Do you mean to tell me that my wife is not my wife?
Larose Here in France, monsieur—the Princess Mathilde is still unmarried.
Mme Blum Two honeymoons and not married ... (*Turning on Charteris*) Sacre-bleu! What have you done to ma princesse?
Charteris Monsieur Larose, this is an outrage.
Larose The law is the law, monsieur. Now, madame, perhaps you will be good enough to indicate to me the Princess Mathilde?
Mme Blum No, monsieur, never!
Larose Very well, madame. (*To the Mannequins*) Mamselles, this way. You will line up please.

Larose indicates a line-up identity parade. They do so. During the following, Jeremiah sneaks under one of the tables with Mme Blum's poodles and a plate of food

Your name?

He asks each until most have been asked. All answer with a false or ludicrous name

(*Eventually realizing and turning to Mme Blum and Charteris*) Madame, monsieur! The penalties for obstructing an officer of the law are severe. I demand to know ...

He sees something moving under one of the tables, which is covered to the ground by a tablecloth

There is something moving over there. (*To a Gendarme*) You! Search the table!

The gendarme does so. Jeremiah is under it feeding tit-bits to the poodles

Mme Blum Ah, my babies!
Larose Sacre-bleu!

No. 17 Finaletto (Act II Scene 1)

All (*singing*)   Ah ha, Monsieur Larose,
We honour and admire you,
But must suggest your taking a rest,
Your noble work must tire you.
And though our window shows
The very latest dresses
We haven't got a suitable lot
Of runaway princesses!
We'll get you some, if you propose
Again to come, Monsieur Larose.
Ah ha, Monsieur Larose,
You grieve us when you leave us!
Ah ha, ah ha, ah ha, ah ha, Monsieur Larose.

Larose (*shouting*) Search the racecourse!

Larose exits with the Gendarmes. Prince Carlo enters

Prince
  (*singing*)   Ah, madame!
Here I am. To invite La Quakeresse.
  (*To Prudence*) May I pray, you will say,
As you answer, only "Yes".
Will you not come to the ball,
Listen and answer the call?
Beautiful girls will be there to dance
All that is fairest and best in France
If you will come to the ball
You shall be queen of them all.
No-one so fair will be there,
At the ball, at the ball.
Prudence   Really, your Highness,
Though you are kind,
Quakerish shyness
Troubles my mind.
I am no dancer

Act II, Scene 1   47

               I cannot go
               So I can answer nothing but no.
Chorus   Her only answer is no!

Larose enters. The following dialogue is spoken over the music

Larose (*addressing Prince Carlo*) Your Highness. I ask your assistance, in the name of the law.
Prince Certainly, Larose—but how?
Larose The Princess Mathilde—to whom your Highness was betrothed—is here.
Prince The Princess Mathilde—here?
Larose Here amongst these girls. I ask you to identify her.
Prudence No! No!
Prince Ah but, mamselle, you refuse to come to the ball.
Prudence I am sorry, monsieur, but I—I cannot.
Prince Then I see no reason for refusing to do as Larose asks.

The girls line up again. Prince Carlo passes in front of them. He stops at Mathilde and looks meaningfully at Prudence

Prudence Your Highness, I shall be delighted to come to your ball!
Prince (*to Larose*) The Princess Mathilde is not here, monsieur.

Larose exits angrily

Chorus
(*singing*)   Ah, she will come to the ball
                 Listen and answer the call.
                 Fair is the fate of the prince's friend,
                 Queen of the Dance to the dance's end!
                 Ah, let us come to the ball,
                 Hailing her queen of us all.
Prince   Ah, you will come to the ball
                 Listen and answer the call.
                 I will be ever your faithful friend,
                 You are my queen 'til the world shall end!
                 Now you will come to the ball,
                 You shall be queen of us all.

Tony enters

Tony (*speaking*) Are you going to this ball, in spite of your promise to me?
Prudence Yes, but you don't understand——
Tony I understand—I understand perfectly well.

Tony exits

Chorus (*singing*) No-one so fair will be there
                      At the ball, at the ball.

A gauze frontcloth is flown in and Prudence moves downstage of it. The Lights fade behind the gauze as No. 17 ends. Immediately the music for No. 18 begins so that the two numbers run on from one another

SCENE 2

On the way back from the races. Immediately following

No. 18 There's Plenty of Love in the World

Prudence (*singing*) Some girls weep when love goes by,
What care I, what care I?
Love has wings so I let him fly,
It's foolish to follow after.
He has gone and I don't know why,
What care I, what care I?
Life is happy and hope is high, hope is high,
With all of the days for laughter.

> Heigh ho, let love go
> With his rosy wings unfurled,
> Soon there will be
> Others for me;
> There is plenty of love in the world.
> Ah, let him go with his wings unfurled,
> Soon there will be
> Others for me;
> There is plenty of love in the world,
> In the world, in the world.

Some girls, sorrow and weep and sigh,
What care I, what care I?
I'm not going to pine and die,
If somebody does not love me.
When a fancy has gone awry,
What care I, what care I?
I've the earth and the sea and sky, sea and sky,
And laugh to the sun above me.

> Heigh ho, let love go
> With his rosy wings unfurled,
> Soon there will be
> Others for me
> There is plenty of love in the world.
> Ah, let him go with his wings unfurled,
> Soon there will be
> Others for me
> There is plenty of love in the world,
> In the world, in the world.

The frontcloth is flown out

Act II, Scene 3

SCENE 3

Prince Carlo's Ball in the Gardens of the Pré-Catalan *Restaurant. That evening*

The Lights come up on the gardens of the Pré-Catalan, *a fashionable restaurant in the Bois de Boulogne. A few tables and chairs surround a central area where the Guests, including Prince Carlo, are dancing. Tony and Diane are seated at a table downstage. Everyone is in fancy dress*

No. 19 Dance

At the end of the dance, a Waiter enters from the restaurant

Waiter Mesdames, messieurs, supper is served.

Some of the Guests exit into the restaurant with the Waiter. Jeremiah and Phoebe enter

Jeremiah Eh—this is something like! Now I know what they mean by gay Paree.
Phoebe Are we going to go and have some more of that bubbly stuff, Jerry, like we had at the princess's wedding?
Jeremiah That's funny, bubbly always makes me think of weddings too.
Phoebe Does it? Then come along and have some!

Phoebe and Jeremiah exit

Diane gets up from her table

Tony You go ahead of me, Diane. I'm not hungry at the moment.
Prince (*coming forward*) Then perhaps you will allow me to escort you, Mamselle Diane?
Diane Why thank you, Highness.

They start to exit

  Has the Quaker girl arrived?
Prince Not yet.
Diane Do you think she will keep her promise and come?
Prince You may rest assured on that, Mamselle—she will be here.

Prince Carlo and Diane exit

Tony, in a dream, sings

No. 20 Just a Friend

Tony Although she's a Quaker, I'll never forsake her—I love her.
  Her "thees" and her "thous" have become a part of my life.
  She's sweet and kind and as bright as the starlight above her,
  She's beautiful—and I'm aiming to make her my wife.
    A friend, she is—as flawless as a fragrant Quaker rose—
    As faithful as a friend could ever be to me.
    But I can't make her see

That I'm in love with her.
A friend, she is, but I would like to make her something more;
To hold her in my arms for ever and a day, and then to softly say:
"You are my friend for life."
She's "Pru", and she sets my heart abeating.
So true, that the spell that she casts—holds me so fast.
I'm in her power, each waking hour, but
A friend, she is—just that, and nothing more, she'll ever be,
I guess she'll never really be a mate for me.
She'll never wait for me.
But I shall dream and hope and pray
That she'll love me the Quaker way,
And friendship may become a dream come true.

Tony slowly exits at the end of the song. As he does so, Larose enters

1st Guest Good-evening, Monsieur Larose.
2nd Guest Looking for more princesses, Monsieur?

The Guests laugh. Larose ignores them

Duhamel enters from the restaurant and approaches Larose

Duhamel Good-evening, Larose. Have you found the Princess Mathilde yet?
Larose No, monsieur. But I shall—I shall.
Duhamel Our famous Larose outwitted by our equally famous Mme Blum. I'm afraid Paris will laugh for a week, and nothing kills in Paris like ridicule you know.
Larose Quite so, monsieur, as you yourself may soon discover.
Duhamel I don't understand.
Larose An innocent liaison with a distinguished lady of the stage ... ?
Duhamel Diane?
Larose Certain letters written to her in idle moments of relaxation from the cares of State?
Duhamel What are you suggesting, Larose?
Larose Monsieur, I suggest nothing.
Duhamel These letters you speak of were merely foolish nonsense—the sort of thing a man may write to any pretty woman.
Larose Of course, monsieur, but as you justly observe, in Paris, nothing kills like ridicule.
Duhamel (*after a pause*) I must have those letters back, Larose. Do you understand? I rely on you.
Larose And I, monsieur, rely on you.
Duhamel For what?
Larose While the Princess Mathilde is free, *I* am laughed at. Do I make myself clear?
Duhamel Very well, Larose. I'll see what can be done.

Act II, Scene 3   51

Mme Blum enters

Mme Blum Ah, bonsoir, messieurs.
Duhamel Bonsoir, Mme Blum.
Larose (*icily*) Madame.

Larose exits

Mme Blum (*watching Larose go*) Oh dear, I am afraid that the inspector will never forgive me for this afternoon. But, monsieur, it is you I came to see. Monsieur, I ask your pardon—pardon for ma princesse—you must allow her to remarry in France.
Duhamel (*with a shrug*) Madame ...
Mme Blum But consider, monsieur—two honeymoons at Barbizon and only half-married. The whole affair is terrible!
Duhamel Madame, I regret I can do nothing.

Duhamel bows politely and exits

Mme Blum (*to the audience*) Oh, merde! (*Following Duhamel off*) But, monsieur, there must be something you can do ...

Mme Blum exits. Prudence, Mathilde and Charteris enter

Prudence You aren't going to leave me here alone, are you?
Mathilde Of course not—we will take care of you.
Charteris But for you my wife might now be under arrest.
Prudence I have come to this ball because I said I would—but I shall stay only for a short while.
Charteris I believe Monsieur Duhamel is here. I'm going to ask him to let the princess stay in France long enough to get married again.
Prudence He told me I might ask any favour of him.
Charteris }
Mathilde   } (*together*) He did?
Prudence Yes. And I have something to give him. Some letters which Mamselle Diane gave to me by mistake. You'll see—everything will turn out right for you. As for me, I'm afraid Tony will never forgive me for coming here.
Charteris The prince is coming! We must go and find Duhamel. We shan't be far away, Prudence.

Mathilde and Charteris exit. Prince Carlo enters

Prince Ah, mamselle, at last—a thousand times welcome!
Prudence Your Highness. I have come as I promised.
Prince And now that you are here, mamselle, I shall do my utmost to entertain you. I hope you will enjoy the ball.
Prudence I am sure I shall. It must be lovely to be a prince, and spend every evening like this.
Prince For me, there has never been an evening like this, mamselle. Will you give me my first dance?
Prudence (*evasively*) Oh, I'm afraid Quakers don't dance, monsieur.

Prince Then at least Quakers take supper?
Prudence (*laughing*) Oh, sometimes, but not as princes do.
Prince I have a table where we shall be quite alone.
Prudence Oh, but first, I must find Mme Blum. Perhaps I may join you in a moment or two?
Prince Certainly, mamselle, I shall await you with impatience.

Prince Carlo exits

Prudence watches him go

Mme Blum enters

Mme Blum Ah, chérie. I have looked everywhere for you. Monsieur Duhamel comes this way. To me he will not listen, but perhaps if you speak with him, hein?
Prudence Yes, of course.
Mme Blum Ah bien! But he must not see me. Good fortune, my little Quaker girl. You bring luck I know. (*She kisses her*) Now, Blum must disappear—voilà!

Mme Blum exits. Duhamel enters

Duhamel Mamselle, I have looked everywhere for you.
Prudence Monsieur, I was looking for you.
Duhamel Indeed!
Prudence I am going to ask you something which you have refused all others, monsieur.
Duhamel So much the better. It will prove, mamselle, that I can refuse you nothing.
Prudence Then, please, *please* let my friend the Princess Mathilde stay in France.
Duhamel Mamselle, I beg you to ask me anything but that.
Prudence But there is nothing else that I have to ask, monsieur.
Duhamel Then I must break my word, and refuse your request. I am sorry. (*He starts to go*)
Prudence Oh monsieur! I have some letters—they are yours I think. (*She hands him the letters*)
Duhamel My letters? But how did *you* come by them?
Prudence From the lady to whom they are addressed, monsieur.
Duhamel From Mamselle Diane . . .? Ah, I am beginning to understand. You intend to bargain, mamselle? My letters for the princess's freedom, ha?
Prudence Monsieur?
Duhamel I am afraid you choose the wrong person with whom to bargain, mamselle.
Prudence Monsieur. Quakers do not traffic in such things. I brought your letters here tonight to return them to you. That is all.
Duhamel And you give them back to me without condition?
Prudence Certainly, monsieur. I am happy to have been of service to you. Au revoir, monsieur. (*She starts to go*)

Act II, Scene 3   53

Duhamel Wait, mamselle. Forgive my having misunderstood you. (*After a pause*) I think there may be a way around our little problem. As France's First Minister, I have the authority to grant your request. (*He looks at the letters*) This I do willingly.
Prudence Then the princess may stay?
Duhamel It shall be as you wish.
Prudence Oh, monsieur, how can I thank you?
Duhamel No thanks, mamselle, but some advice. Think of your own happiness as well as that of others. Again I warn you to beware of the prince.
Prudence Oh monsieur, I do not even think of the prince, but of someone else.
Duhamel Ah, mamselle, I am still young enough to be envious of "someone else". Now, I must find the Chief of Police and tell him that he may call off his search for the princess.

He bows, and is about to take his leave when Prudence kisses him on the cheek

Duhamel exits bashfully

Prudence Oh, I'm so happy. I should like to dance—just as Tony taught me. My Tony from America. (*She sings*)

No. 21   Tony from America

All along the garden where the moonbeams glance,
    Music echoes loud and clear,
Girls have got their partners for the joyous dance,
    But the one I want's not here!
There are partners made in Germany and Gentlemen of France,
There are boys who come from England, but they haven't any chance
    With
Tony, from America!
Over the sea,
He guessed I was all alone
So that's why he came along and found me!
    Over in America
    Some day we'll be,
When a cottage we have rented
    We'll be quite contented,
Tony and me!

All along the pathway of the summer moon,
    He is coming now, I know,
He is out to find me and he'll meet me soon,
    Whisper to me soft and low.
There are girls who blush and smile at him
    And try to win his heart,

For they want him very badly, but I never want to part
   With
Tony from America!
Over the sea.
He guessed I was all alone
So that's why he came along and found me!
   Over in America
   Some day we'll be,
When a cottage we have rented
   We'll be quite contented,
   Tony and me!

She dances

When a cottage we have rented
   We'll be quite contented,
   Tony and me!

Tony enters

Tony So you did come? In spite of your promise?
Prudence I was obliged to come, friend Tony.
Tony Obliged? Obliged to break your word?
Prudence Thou dost not understand.
Tony Oh, I understand all right.
Prudence If thou wilt listen.
Tony Listen? The man who listens to a woman is a fool. You've fooled me once already—and now you try again. I trusted you, Prudence.
Prudence Is that why you followed me here?
Tony I *came* here because I couldn't believe you'd break your word.
Prudence Thou hast doubts of me?
Tony I believe what my eyes tell me. You're here—that's enough. You pretended you loved me, and yet you put yourself at the beck and call of the first man that flatters you.
Prudence (*gently*) Thou dost not flatter me, friend. My coming here tonight was the price of the prince's silence this afternoon. Otherwise he would have identified the Princess Mathilde to the Chief of Police.
Tony You did that to save Mathilde?
Prudence I didn't think it too great a price to pay—until I tasted the bitterness of your doubt.
Tony (*after an embarrassed pause*) What a prize idiot! But, understand, my anger was only concern for you in the hands of the prince. Why, he's the most notorious——

She kisses him

   I take it I'm forgiven? I promise I'll try not to jump to hasty conclusions in future. I'll improve when I get ...

Act II, Scene 3   55

Prudence Wisdom?
Tony No—when I get Prudence.

No. 22 The First Dance

Prudence	Thee loves me and I love thee
	Love's the only true marriage-maker.
	Thy little wife I'm going to be
	And not the little wife of a Quaker.
Tony	Though you have been asked by many.
	I see!
Prudence	Just to take a step, take a step, take a step!
Tony	You shall never dance with any but me!
Prudence	Let us take a step, take a step, take a step!
Tony	All in vain the rest besought you tonight!
Prudence	Just to take a step, take a step, take a step!
Tony	Now we'll do the dance I taught you.
Both	All right!

They polka

Mme Blum, Mathilde and Charteris enter

Mathilde Prudence, have you seen Monsieur Duhamel?
Prudence Yes, it's all settled. You are free to stay in France.

Jeremiah and Phoebe enter during the following

Mme Blum Bravo! Well done my little Quaker girl. (*Referring to Tony*) And you have the reward for your good work.
Tony Oh, I'm the one who has the reward. And I'm going to make sure I don't lose it this time. Do you have another wedding dress, Mme Blum?
Mme Blum Ah, chérie, congratulations.

Everyone congratulates Prudence and Tony

Charteris Congratulations, dear chap!
Jeremiah Better make it two dresses, madame! (*He holds up Phoebe's left hand which has a ring on it*)

A further round of mutual congratulations

Larose enters

Larose Ah ha! The Princess Mathilde, at last, I think! Pardon, madame—voilà! (*He produces a warrant*) I have here, madame, a warrant for your immediate exile from France.

Duhamel enters

Duhamel Just one moment, Larose, I've been looking for you. The princess has been granted leave to remain here. The English marriage was perfectly valid—even in France. So this lady is no longer the Princess Mathilde, but Mrs Charteris—an English subject.

Larose (*brokenly*) But—I ...
Duhamel I am genuinely sorry, Larose.

Larose drops back, dejected and defeated. He sits

And now, mesdames, messieurs. I think we should reveal the events of this evening to the prince. Would you please follow me?

Duhamel exits, followed by the Guests, Mathilde, Charteris, Tony, Prudence, Jeremiah and Phoebe

Mme Blum starts to follow them off then she turns, looks at Larose and approaches him

Mme Blum Inspector ...

Larose doesn't look up

Monsieur Larose ... Hercule ...

He looks up

This has not been a good day for you, hein?
Larose I am the laughing stock of Paris, madame, thanks to you—and your poodles.
Mme Blum But, monsieur—understand—I could not let you exile ma petite princess, who I have known and loved since she was a baby.
Larose Madame—the law is the law!
Mme Blum (*trying to get round him*) Oh come, Hercule. Have some wine and soon this cauchemar will be forgotten. For tonight, think only of pleasant things, hein? The stars ... the music ... the wine ... everywhere ... everyone ... L'amour! Oh Hercule, do not fight it! You know, I'm not sure if it is the wine, but I feel a foolish sort of feeling coming on. Ah, oui, but of course, it is the night of the new moon—that explains everything! (*She sings*)

No. 23   Moonstruck

Moon, moon, mischief-making moon!
What are you doing there?
You seem like a fairy dream
Up in the midnight air.
When I look at you I always know
You will shoot me with your silver bow.
Just as soon as the daylight's gone,
Well, it's then I feel a foolish sort of feeling coming on.

I'm such a silly when the moon comes out
I hardly seem to know what I'm about
Skipping, hopping, never, never stopping.
I can't keep still although I try.
I'm all aquiver when the moonbeams glance,
That is the moment when I long to dance.
I can never close a sleepy eye
When the moon comes creeping up the sky.

Act II, Scene 3

Larose Moon, moon, aggravating moon
Why do you tease me so?
I think you're inclined to wink
That isn't right, you know.
Mme Blum Everyday I'll be as good as gold.
Doing everything that I am told
But as soon as the sun's in bed,
Well, it's then I've such a flighty little foolish little head.

I'm such a silly when the moon comes out
I hardly seem to know what I'm about
Skipping, hopping, never, never stopping.
I can't keep still although I try.
I'm all aquiver when the moonbeams glance,
That is the moment when I long to dance.
I can never close a sleepy eye
When the moon comes creeping up the sky.

They dance a tango, followed by the can-can

Finally they are joined by a chorus of Waiters for the climax to the number

Waiters She's all aquiver when the moonbeams glance,
That is the moment when she longs to dance,
She can never close a sleepy eye
When the moon comes creeping, slyly peeping,
Moon comes creeping up the sky.

Prince Carlo, Diane, Prudence, Tony, Charteris, Mathilde, Jeremiah, Phoebe and the Company enter

Prince (*to Prudence*) Well, mamselle, it seems I must accept a gracious defeat. You realize that my reputation is in ruins. To lose one lady is bad enough, but two is nothing short of a disaster.

All laugh

No matter. At least Mamselle Diane does not desert me. And now, please, I ask only one thing: that you enjoy the remainder of this ball, and that our next dance be led by the toast of Paris—Miss Prudence, The Quaker Girl.

No. 24 Finale

All (*singing*) Ah, Paris,
That is the place to see,
For love and song and life and light,
And laughter all the day and night,
Ah, Paris,
Merry and gay and free!
The flower of earth, the mother of mirth!
Paris, Paris, Paris!

CURTAIN

FURNITURE AND PROPERTY LIST

ACT I

SCENE 1

On stage: Oak tree with bench

Off stage: Car containing suitcases and several hatboxes
Glass of gin and ginger beer **(William)**
Tray containing glasses, wine, jug of water **(William)**

Personal: **Tony:** brooch in pocket
Charteris: watch
Prudence: book
Jeremiah: cigar, box of matches

SCENE 2

On stage: Nil

SCENE 3

On stage: Tailor's dummies
Table. *On it:* mail, etc.
Chairs
Mirror

Personal: **Mathilde:** letter
Jeremiah: fancy garter
Diane: parasol
Newspaper Reporters: notebooks, pencils
Prudence: letter

ACT II

SCENE 1

On stage: Tables. *On them:* large tablecloths, glasses, bottles of wine, food etc.
Chairs

Off stage: Banknotes **(Jeremiah)**
Bundle of letters **(Diane)**

SCENE 2

On stage: Nil

Personal: **Prudence:** bundle of letters
Phoebe: engagement ring on finger
Larose: warrant

LIGHTING PLOT

Property fittings required: nil
Interior and exterior settings

ACT I, SCENE 1. Exterior
To open: Bright sunshine effect
No cues

ACT I, SCENE 2. Exterior
To open: General lighting downstage
No cues

ACT I, SCENE 3. Interior
To open: Full general lighting
No cues

ACT II, SCENE 1. Exterior
To open: Bright sunshine effect
Cue 1   As frontcloth is flown in   (Page 47)
          Crossfade to lighting on downstage area

ACT II, SCENE 2. Exterior
To open: Downstage area lit
No cues

ACT II, SCENE 3. Exterior
To open: Evening effect with artificial lights on dance area
No cues

EFFECTS PLOT

ACT I

Cue 1	**Charteris:** "You'll like him a lot." *Car engine approaching. Cut when ready*	(Page 7)
Cue 2	**Rachel:** "... in the paths of waywardness." *Clatter of dishes being dropped*	(Page 8)
Cue 3	At the end of song No. 6 *Wedding bells*	(Page 17)

ACT II

No cues

www.ingramcontent.com/pod-product-compliance
Ingram Content Group UK Ltd.
Pitfield, Milton Keynes, MK11 3LW, UK
UKHW021842140426
5217IPUK00022B/1553

9 780573 080807